Muskegon 365

Muskegon 365

The All-Season Guide to Michigan's West Coast

Roger Rapoport

RDR Books
Muskegon, Michigan

Muskegon 365

RDR Books
1487 Glen Avenue
Muskegon, MI 49441
phone: 510-595-0595
fax: 510-228-0300
www.rdrbooks.com
email: read@rdrbooks.com

ISBN: 978-1-57143-170-7
Library of Congress Control Number: 2008923331

Design and production: Richard Harris
Photos: courtesy of Muskegon County
Convention and Visitors Bureau
Additional color photography: Dan Rapoport

Distributed in the United Kingdom and Europe by
Roundhouse Publishing Ltd., Millstone, Limers Lane,
Northam, North Devon EX39 2RG, United Kingdom

Distributed in Canada by
Scholarly Book Services, 127 Portland Street, 3rd Floor,
Toronto, Ontario, Canada M5V 2N4

Printed in the United States of America

CONTENTS

Introduction 1

Lodging 21

Downtown Muskegon 32

Muskegon's Great Outdoors 52

Sports and Recreation 77

Lakeside District and the Channel 93

Seafaring 96

Music and Entertainment 105

Muskegon's Big Events 114

Shopping Guide 125

Restaurant Guide 134

White Lake Area 150

Weddings 156

Michigan's Adventure and
   WildWater Adventure 166

Schools 172

Religious Life 177

Muskegon's Economy 183

Acknowledgements 188

Contributors 189

Index 191

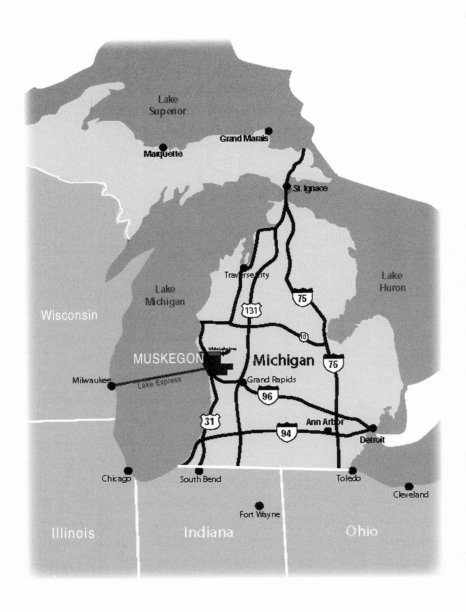

(Maps of Muskegon County and Downtown Muskegon appear on pp. 34–35)

INTRODUCTION

Michigan boasts many big-name destinations such as Mackinac Island, Traverse City, Ann Arbor and Frankenmuth, yet Michigan's "West Coast" is one of the best kept secrets in the American heartland. True, the region has never been a superstar on hot lists of travel destinations. And even if you've previously visited Muskegon, you may not know all the region's best bets, hidden hideaways or local favorites. If you live here, chances are much of what you are about to discover in these pages will reconfirm the wisdom of your decision to make this region your home. People who already know about the area's beaches, lakes and rivers, its parks, festivals and cultural centers, restaurants and bed and breakfasts will also find their knowledge broadened by this book. Sailors, kayakers, runners, bikers, golfers, fishermen and women, and cross-skiers take note: you can enjoy the great outdoors 365 days a year at a fraction of the cost you'd expect to pay at brand-name tourist hot spots.

This insiders guide will show you how fast this region is changing for the better. Even as we put the finishing touches on this book, our editorial team keeps turning up delightful new places. Fortunately, with our handy web update you'll never be more than a few clicks away from the latest details that will keep this breaking story up to date.

With beauty to take your breath away, entertainment and music all around and a wealth of opportunities for exciting adventures, you really do have to look more than surface deep to find the true treasures in Muskegon. This book opens the door to many of the reasons why you may want to consider Muskegon—the largest deep water port on the eastern shore of Lake Michigan and home to incredible all-season trails and parks—as your headquarters for a traditional summer holiday or an off-season getaway.

Muskegon, the White Lake area and their neighbors offer year-round opportunities for just about any kind of vacation. From sailing and fishing to arts and leisure, amusement parks, the cross-lake ferry, restaurants, beachcombing, kayaking, windsurfing, swimming, farm tours, bird watching, fall color loops, historic museums and art galleries, this region is a winner.

Perfect for cycling and running, Muskegon also offers advantages many people overlook when choosing a vacation spot. A safe community where every beach comes with a money-back, shark-free guarantee, Muskegon is blessed with nationally recognized medical centers (in case you stub your toe on the boardwalk). For more than 25 million Midwest residents, this region is less than a day's ride away. Muskegon is far less expensive and easier to navigate than competing resort areas. With the added plus of relatively mild summer weather, it's no wonder so many sailors from other regions harbor their boats here. Unlike much of the surrounding region, prevailing breezes off Lake Michigan help to moderate temperatures and humidity. In the winter, temperatures are often warmer than inland communities as well.

Seasoned travelers and big city residents expect to get stuck in monster traffic jams on Friday night, but Muskegon will surprise you. Although 175,000 residents call this county home, traffic tie-ups are a rarity even during peak holiday times. While hotels and cottages fill up quickly during the height of summer, the region is blessed with plenty of other options at reasonable prices. During much of the year, lodging is priced well below competing resorts that require more drive time. Readers who prefer the convenience of flying will be pleased to know that the local airport was voted number one in a pilot/flight attendant poll conducted by Northwest's regional airline, Mesaba.

Given all these advantages, you might wonder why Muskegon remains relatively undiscovered. As you'll learn in the pages ahead, unlike many other resort areas, this community has controlled development to make sure that its many advantages are protected for future generations. For example, unlike many other beach resorts that have succumbed to the temptation of helter-skelter development projects, Muskegon has protected much of its shoreline with a network of waterfront parks that guarantee access for everybody. You don't have to worry about high-rises blocking sunset views or smog filling the clean lakeside air.

Because the county has more than 15 miles of public Lake Michigan access, as well as idyllic inland lakes ideal for boating, fishing and swimming, you won't have to compete for elbow room on some of the finest beaches in the world. Many local residents choose Muskegon's beaches for their clean, sugarlike sand and water and ample breathing room. Backed up by gorgeous dunes, beaches in the region are blessedly free of rocky shorelines. Safe, clean waterfronts are ideal for small children and families. A number of lakes feature "no wake" zones so you don't have to worry about sharing the water with fast moving power boats. And with many lakefront parks, it's usually just minutes from your campsite to the water.

Muskegon 365 is the first comprehensive guidebook to the Muskegon area. As our editorial team—Louis Jeannot, Laura Mazade, Rowena McKenzie, Sarah Meinel, Rachel Moblo, Kellie Norman, Jessi Prouse, Mike Schertenlieb, Abby Schmeling, Sara Sheehan, Megan Trank, Colleen Weesies and myself—visited restaurants, bed and break-fasts, hotels, cottages, lakefront resorts, moderately priced campgrounds, motels and inns, parks, bike paths, lakes, streams, cultural centers and amusement park thrill rides, we've often found ourselves wondering why nobody has done a book like this before.

We've learned that for all its charms, Muskegon has been a place that is reluctant to oversell itself. In an era of hype, this is a community that focuses on offering dependable value with an emphasis on comfort and safety. Sure, the city could charge for parking; the lack of pay parking meters says a lot about a community that works hard not to nickel and dime citizens or visitors. Muskegon has demonstrated great care in its development efforts, remaining protective of its natural resources and remarkable environmental as-sets. When something exciting is added to the tourist mix, such as the high-speed *Lake Express* ferry to Milwaukee, it's done right. Just ask the passengers who have turned this business gamble into a success story.

Go ahead, unfasten your seat belt and get ready for a journey that literally turns back the clock on vacation life. Discover a place where you can relax without standing in line or elbowing your way to happiness. Now just head out to one of Muskegon's picture-perfect beaches and come on in. The water is fine, and you won't have to worry about parking fines.

MUSKEGON OVERVIEW

An ideal beach resort, with wonderful dunes offering miles of serene hiking, Muskegon makes it easy to slow down and forget the hassles of large metropolitan areas. You'll certainly want to check out the coastline, possibly the area's greatest asset. In a state with more than 2,000 miles of coastline, this community has done an extraordinary job of protecting its waterfront. We recommend getting out of your car as soon as possible. Whether you walk, sail or head out in a power boat, bike, kayak or canoe, you'll quickly discover that the secret to a great trip is to play outdoors, even in the winter. Around the seasons, you can enjoy long bike rides through idyllic farmland, cross-country ski in the Hoffmaster dunes or Muskegon State Park, hike through fall color hot spots, sail Lake Michigan at sunset or simply stroll among historic landmarks downtown. Muskegon offers a variety of cultural treasures including the Richardsonian Romanesque Hackley Public Library, the Muskegon

Museum of Art, the impressive Hackley and Hume homes, and the vital and diverse Muskegon County Museum.

In the evenings you'll be surprised by the variety of cultural happenings within an hour of downtown Muskegon. In fact, if you plan your trip carefully, chances are you'll be able to catch celebrity entertainers for far less than you might pay in a big city. The acoustics are outstanding at some of the region's favorite performance venues, such as the venerable Frauenthal Theater, one of the finest in the state.

A short drive into the Manistee National Forest takes you to an affordable summer-long concert series featuring world-class classical performers at Blue Lake Fine Arts Camp, one of the nation's leading summer arts communities. These $5 concerts feature virtuosos as well as promising newcomers who are trained at the music camp where jazz great James Carter and members of the Philadelphia Orchestra and the Los Angeles Philharmonic got their start. 300 East Crystal Lake Road, Twin Lake. (800) 221-3796. www.bluelake.org

PLANNING YOUR TRIP TO MUSKEGON

If you are unsure where to start, two great leads are the *Muskegon Chronicle* and WBLV, the 100,000-watt FM station operated by Blue Lake Fine Arts Camp. Both offer extensive coverage of forthcoming arts events, and you can check them out online before you arrive. Another reliable information resource is www.visitmuskegon.org or Muskegon. org. Watch closely when you are in town; Muskegon does not always hype its greatest hits. Planning ahead can insure that you don't miss "best bets" during your visit.

In midsummer, cottages are hard to book, and local events like the Muskegon Summer Celebration flood the area with excited music lovers who can't resist an 11-day concert schedule for just $99. (No, that is not a misprint). Even on relatively uneventful summer weekends, local accommodations can fill up quickly. Although Muskegon County has more than 1,200 campsites, holiday weekends are tricky. You'll want to book far ahead during the peak summer season so you won't risk showing up at your camp-site of choice and getting turned away. It's smart to make rental reservations for boats, canoes, kayaks and bikes well ahead, too.

During your visit you'll want to set aside time to kick back. With Muskegon's relaxing pace, we consider down-time a no-brainer. During the summer months, plan to slow down in the late afternoon, when the heat peaks. Since Muskegon is at the western edge of the eastern time zone, you'll be able to enjoy the evening light as late as 10:00 p.m. At other times of year it makes more sense to get an early start, because darkness comes early, greeting you for dinner in the deepest days of winter.

Muskegon enjoys a relatively low crime rate, but for your safety we recommend carrying a cell phone, leaving contact information with family members, using a good map and never letting children (especially small children) out of your sight. Please do not entrust the safety of your children to peo-ple you don't know. Parents may want to consider bringing along their own babysitter, someone who knows the children and has earned the parents' trust. The YMCA of Muskegon and the Hackley Library both offer children's activities that may help to free up alone time for adults.

Child safety is especially important on the beach. Don't be fooled by the tranquility of the lake; in Michigan, conditions near the water can change in minutes. Locals generally know it is best to expect the unexpected. No matter how much experience you have with the water, the Muskegon area's relatively safe beaches and sandy bottoms typically come without lifeguards. Don't swim alone. Rely on the buddy system at all times. And don't forget, cold Lake Michigan water temperatures present a risk of hypothermia.

If you have a GPS navigation system or are using Mapquest, back it up with a printed road map and careful written directions. You might even want to consider calling for directions. Even the best technology needs a backup, especially on the beaches, where cell phone reception can be spotty.

Now, if you're ready, let the grand tour begin.

MUSKEGON WEATHER

Because Michigan is located in the northern Midwest, Muskegon is a true four-season environment ideal for every kind of sport. Average high temperatures during the winter months (December to March) are between 30 and 45 degrees Fahrenheit, with lows between 17 and 25 degrees. Muskegon tends to receive significant lake-effect snow, making conditions ideal for winter sports such as skiing and snowboarding. Fall and spring temperatures are balmier, ranging from lows of 35 to 55 degrees, to highs of 55 to 75 degrees. With light, crisp air, these are some of the best days in the area. Summer months, between June and September, average between 60 and 80. Inland lakes have average surface temperatures of 65 degrees during the summer. Cold Lake Michigan water temperatures may mean you'll want to reduce your swimming time, taking breaks to warm up.

We strongly recommend against outdoor activities after dark, particularly biking, ORVing, hunting or aquatic activities such as swimming, boating, fishing or hunting. And it goes without saying that alcohol does not mix well with any of these activities, particularly those that involve water sports or boating. If you're new to the area, inquire locally for information about changing conditions, road construction or threatening weather.

MUSKEGON ABCs

There are four easy ways to reach Muskegon.

By Car
- *Locally:* Muskegon is reached via US 31 from the north and the south.
- *From the Chicago area:* Take the Skyway to the Indiana Tollway (90), then hop on I-94 north to Michigan where you can catch US 31 north, near Benton Harbor.
- *From eastern Michigan:* I-96 connects directly from Grand Rapids, Lansing and Detroit.
- *From the I-90 Indiana tollway:* take US 31 north at South Bend.

By Air

Mesaba Airlines, a Northwest commuter airline, connects to Muskegon through Detroit. (800) 225-2525 or (231) 733-3107. **Midwest** offers jet service through Milwaukee. (800) 452-2022.

Just five miles from downtown, the **Muskegon County Airport** is a pleasant alternative to overcrowded terminals. The convenient parking lot is a bargain. In the winter months, customers are often stunned to discover that snow has been removed from their cars by friendly employees who even draw happy faces on their windshields. Primarily for light private aircraft, this general aviation airport also offers charter flights on a 24-hour basis through **Executive Air Transport**, (231) 798-2126. www.ea-transport.com

The **Gerald R. Ford International Airport**, 50 miles southeast of Muskegon in Grand Rapids, provides nonstop flights to Eastern, Midwestern and Southern cities. Carriers include Northwest, Midwest, American, United, Delta, and Continental.

Chicago's **O'Hare** and **Midway** airports are three to four hours by car from Muskegon, depending on traffic and time of day. A shuttle bus service from both airports goes to **Michigan City, Indiana**, just two hours south of Muskegon via US 31 south and I-94 west, where you can rent a car for the trip north. This approach avoids Chicago bottlenecks. You can also park your car here at no charge, which easily offsets the bus fare. See Transit Alternatives below for more details.

By Ferry

May through early November, the high-speed *Lake Express* ferry offers daily service between Muskegon and Milwaukee. Car deck space is limited; reservations are strongly recommended. The scenic trip takes just two hours and 30 minutes. (866) 914-1010. www.lakeexpress.com. If car reservations on the *Lake Express* are a problem, consider parking your car at your departure point and picking up an inexpensive rental on the other side of the lake. If you must travel by car and can't find space on the *Lake Express*, consider the larger **SS Badger** from Manitowoc, Wisconsin to Ludington, 60 miles north of Muskegon. The trip takes four hours (800) 841-4243. www.ssbadger.com. Using both ferries makes a nice loop trip.

By Train
Amtrak's Pere Marquette offers daily evening service from Chicago to Holland, 35 miles south of Muskegon. The train departs from Holland daily at 8:21 a.m. and arrives in Chicago at 10:30 a.m. Reservations are strongly advised. The return trip leaves Chicago at 5:20 p.m. and reaches Holland at 9:20 p.m., so you'll need to arrange a ride or spend the night (Holland is a pleasant resort town) and rent a car the following morning. (800) USARAIL or www.amtrak.com.

By Bus
Greyhound offers daily service to and from Grand Rapids, Detroit and Chicago, hubs where you can easily connect to other cities throughout the country and Canada. (800) 231-2222. www.greyhound.com

Rental Car
Major car rental firms serving Muskegon include **Hertz** (231-798-2370 or 231-755-9000), **Avis** (800-331-1212), **Bud-**

get (231-733-1999), **National** (231-798-4758) and **Enterprise** (231-725-8500).

Local Transit

Muskegon Area Transit System (MATS) buses and trolleys provide local service throughout the community. (231) 724-6420.

Taxis

You can call a cab at **Port City Cab** (231-739-7161), **Red's Taxi** (213-755-3949) or **Yellow Cab** (231-739-8294).

Bike Rentals

You'll find bicycles for rent at **The Bicycle Rack**, 1790 Robert Street, (231) 773-6411; or **Powers Outdoors** (summer season only), 4253 Dowling Street, Montague, (231) 893-0687.

Transit Alternatives

While Muskegon's airport is a gem, there may be times when you will turn to other airports. Grand Rapids is a good hub, and Holland is an easy way to link in to the Amtrak system. Here are alternatives that are good to keep in mind when weather, flight or train delays force you to look elsewhere.

First, keep in mind that if your flight is cancelled, you can still reach hubs such as Chicago, Detroit or Milwaukee. If you can't get out on another flight, airlines will give you a chance to make your connecting flight through one of these other cities. You may prefer to rent a car (or in the case of a trip to Milwaukee, take the *Lake Express* May through early November). Here are a few easy strategies.

If your Muskegon flight is cancelled, carriers will often let you switch to a flight out of Grand Rapids. If your Grand Rapids flight is cancelled, it's also possible to rebook out of Lansing, an hour farther east. If you are forced to drive to Detroit or Chicago to pick up a flight, here are two ways to cut down on the long trip and avoid traffic congestion and save on parking costs.

Travelers with their own cars headed to O'Hare or Midway can make the two-hour, 120-mile drive down US 31 and I-94 to Michigan City. Coach USA offers hourly connections to both airports at the Michigan City Holiday Inn at US 421 and Keefer Road. Exit 34B off I-94. Service to the airports begins at 4:20 a.m. and ends at 6:20 p.m. If you're coming in from O'Hare or Midway to Michigan, buses leave O'Hare for the return trip starting at 4:50 a.m. and from Midway at 6:15 a.m. Service continues until 11:15 p.m. at both O'Hare and Midway. Parking at the Michigan City Holiday Inn is free and the trip to either airport is two hours and 20 minutes. Fares are $45 roundtrip. For more information call (800) 248-8747.

Travelers to the Detroit Airport can make the 100-mile drive to East Lansing and catch the Michigan Flyer bus to Detroit Metro Airport. Buses with free wireless leave East Lansing beginning at 2:40 a.m. and continue every two hours until 4:30 p.m. Buses return from the Detroit Airport beginning at 6:45 a.m. and continue until 9:20 p.m. Fares are $25 each way, parking costs are minimal. Call (888) 643-5937 or visit www.michiganflyer.com

Although Amtrak has only one early morning train a day to Chicago from Grand Rapids, there is another way to make later connections to points east and south. South

Bend, Indiana, 120 miles down US 31 has good evening connections. The Lake Shore Limited train eastbound, with connections to New York, Boston, Philadelphia, Baltimore, Washington D.C. and many other cities, leaves South Bend at 12:30 a.m. This helps you avoid the long layover for connections in Chicago that force you to leave Holland early in the morning. An earlier option is the Capitol Limited at 9:33 p.m. (be sure to check for schedule changes). You'll also enjoy free parking. Allow extra time to reach the South Bend Amtrak depot at 2702 West Washington Avenue. (800) USARAIL. www.Amtrak.com

Finally, the *Lake Express* is a quick and easy way to hook in to both the airline and Amtrak systems through Milwaukee from May through early November. Some Chicago-bound travelers find it easier to take the ferry to Milwaukee and then pick up a car or take a train in to Chicago. While it costs more, it's a very pleasant ride.

NEWS AND INFORMATION

Muskegon does not have its own television station, and local radio news coverage is limited. This means that the venerable *Muskegon Chronicle*, one of the few newspapers in America that's actually gaining circulation, is the only comprehensive source of news and information. While there are other handy local papers such as the *White Lake Beacon*, the *Chronicle* dominates the market. Besides providing complete coverage of local events—and a daily list of best bets—the *Chronicle* is also a pleasure to read. The paper's editorial page, directed by veteran David Kolb, is first class. Veteran writers such as Susan Harrison Wolffis and Clayton Hardiman are not to be missed. Jeff Alexander is one of the top environmental writers in the region, while the paper's sports section offers encyclopedic coverage of prep sports, a major topic of conversation in the area. Dave Alexander offers good coverage of the local business scene with a focus on promising entrepreneurs who find Muskegon a great place for a startup. The list goes on and on with names like Bill Iddings, the iconoclastic Tracy Lorenz and editor Paul Keep. The Sunday edition is filled with helpful tips that will add to your vacation pleasure. Letters to the editor on Sunday are an endless source of local color. You can visit the *Chronicle* online at www.mlive.com.

For more regional coverage, you may also want to check out the *Grand Rapids Press*. Newshounds will be glad to know that the Detroit and Chicago papers, as well as the *New York Times*, are widely available in Muskegon.

You can pick up maps, visitor's information and an audio walking tour of downtown Muskegon at the **Muskegon County Convention and Visitor's Bureau**, 610 W. Western Avenue, on the lakeshore across from Heritage Landing. In fact, why not make this your first stop on arrival? This great resource is located in Muskegon's Historic Depot, formerly a train station built in the regionally prevalent Romanesque style. The bureau also features a transportation museum with model railroads and historic information. For updated information on virtually any Muskegon area event or attraction, call (800) 250-9283 or visit the bureau's website at www.visitmuskegon.com.

The **Muskegon Chamber of Commerce Welcome Center** offers good general information about the business, government and education sections of the community. This is a great place to visit if you are looking to do business or relocate to the area.

EMERGENCY AND HEALTH CARE

If you need medical care during your visit, Muskegon's Mercy Health Partners, which merged with Hackley Health in 2008, will provide excellent care. First-class emergency care is just minutes away from the region's popular beaches and parks. Long known for the high quality of its medical community, the Muskegon area is blessed with top specialists who love working in this resort area.

Hackley Hospital
Just prior to its merger with Mercy, Hackley Hospital was named to Thomson Healthcare's top 100 hospital list, Hackley has also won a Governor's Award of Excellence for its emergency medical department. The Hackley campus's major services include a cancer center, an 11-suite surgical department, Family Birth Place, the area's only in-patient Psychiatric Hospital, Muskegon's largest Occupational Health Center, and the new Hackley Health at the Lakes campus near the Lakes Mall. This new facility includes offices for primary and urgent care, as well as a women's center providing a wide range of services. Hackley also has a major athletic medicine and rehabilitation center and features a da Vinci robot-assisted surgical technology. 1700 Clinton Street. (231) 726-3511.

Mercy Health Partners

Named as one of Solucient's Top 100 hospitals, Mercy General has also won a HealthGrades Distinguished Hospital Award for Clinical Excellence. Mercy Hospital's services include a birth center, Johnson Family Center for Cancer Care, Center for Weight Management, Lakeshore Aesthetic Laser Centers, emergency center, rehabilitation services, sleep disorders center and pool classes at AquaTherapy. There are two locations: Mercy Campus at 1500 East Sherman Boulevard and Muskegon General Campus at 1700 Oak Avenue. (231) 672-2000.

MUSKEGON TAKES A BOW

Muskegon has won a number of impressive accolades in recent years. *Forbes Magazine* says "Muskegon is top ten in the nation among cities its size for culture and leisure activities."

According to *National Geographic Travel,* "Muskegon/Grand Rapids Area is one of the best places in the nation to live and play." The magazine also placed the area among the top eight in the nation for waterfront communities, highlighting Norton Shores' Hoffmaster State Park as one of the top beach adventures in America.

Health Grades points out that "patients, families and employers here truly have access to health care that is among the best in the nation."

Local Pere Marquette is the only beach in Michigan to win the Certified Blue Wave Clean Beach Award from the Washington, DC-based Clean Beaches Council.

A LOCAL HERO

The name Charles Hackley is synonymous with the city he helped build. This local hero has a library, a park, a hospital and even a day of celebration named in his honor. His bust, found at the entrance to the library, is frequently clad in a bright T-shirt or, in cold weather, a warm hat and muffler. "Charlie" is remembered as an unconventional gent with a great vision and a philanthropic heart.

Born into a working-class Wisconsin family, Hackley began working at the age of 16. When his father moved to Muskegon to work for the lumber yards, Hackley soon followed. He was paid by the value of his work rather than by the hour, soon rising to $25 a month—a good salary at the time and a testament to his strong work ethic.

In the 1850s, after a slump in the lumber industry brought an economic depression, Charles Hackley decided the only way to make a stable living was to purchase a lumber mill and start his own business. Keeping a close eye on the big picture, Hackley recognized the growth potential in the lumber industry and began acquiring mills across the nation. Eventually, Hackley partnered with Thomas Hume to create one of America's largest lumber firms, which remained in business until 1894.

By then the Michigan forests were completely depleted. Hackley looked for ways the lumber industry could be diversified.

The Great Depression would have been devastating had it not been for Hackley's vision. Joining with local businessmen to create what is now the Muskegon Chamber of Commerce, the area was blessed with new enterprises like the Chase Piano Company, Amazon Knitting Company, Continental Motors and Central Paper Company. Besides economic growth, Charles Hackley contributed $6 million to the community for schools, the Hackley Public Library, Hackley Hospital, an art gallery, parks, statues, monuments, welfare and scholarships.

Guided by the principles of Andrew Carnegie's book *Gospel of Wealth*, Hackley believed that money should not just be used to hold up the poor, but also to sustain the efforts of individuals determined to better themselves. Role model, local hero and visionary, Hackley remains an inspiration for a city that benefits from his industriousness every day.

Today the Muskegon Community Foundation continues the Hackley philanthropic tradition. As a publicly supported community endowment, the foundation receives and manages contributions from community citizens and organizations committed to the future of Muskegon County. The foundation supports the arts, education, environment, community development, health and human services as well as youth development issues. www.cffmc.org

MUSKEGON'S BEST BETS

Have limited time for a visit? If you're eager to hit the highlights, here are a few of our best bets.

- Begin with breakfast at the **Cherokee**, a longtime favorite on Sherman Avenue.
- Head downtown to the **Hackley Library** and visit the historic Julia Hackley room, a great place to read the paper or enjoy your favorite magazine.
- Proceed next door to the **Muskegon Museum of Art** and enjoy the outstanding collection and fine gift shop.
- For lunch in good weather we recommend **Dockers Fish House and Lounge**, with its fine marine view.
- A lunch ride on the ***Port City Princess*** is a fantastic way to see the lake.
- If you would prefer to swim at the beach, head for **Duck Lake State Park** south of Whitehall, where you can swim in Lake Michigan or Duck Lake across the street.
- Outdoor buffs may want to consider canoeing or kayaking along the **White River** or renting a sailboat at **Torresen Marine**.
- In colder months, try the **Muskegon Winter Sports Park**.
- Enjoy your dinner next to a fireplace at the **Hearthstone** or savor the seasonal cuisine at the **Sardine Room**.
- Budget diners will enjoy **El Tapatio**.
- In the summer months, an evening concert at **Blue Lake Fine Arts Camp** is a great idea.
- At other times of year, try to catch the West Shore Symphony led by conductor Scott Speck at the **Frauenthal Performing Arts Center**.
- You'll love the events at the **Howmet Playhouse** in Whitehall, a great place for concerts and theater.
- Sports fans will can get a kick out of watching the **Muskegon Fury** hockey team.
- And just about any fair-weather night, a trip out to **Pere Marquette Park** for a drive or walk is a great way to end the day.

LODGING

L odging should be thought of in terms of four major areas: downtown, US 31 access, the lakefronts, and White Lake. Downtown offers the Holiday Inn and the Shoreline Inn and Suites. A cluster of hotels and motels including the Fairfield Inn, the Baymont (formerly AmeriHost) and the Comfort Inn can be found along US 31. Lakefront cottages and the Michillinda Lodge offer Lake Michigan access.

In the White Lake area there are a variety of fine hotels, motels, inns and restaurants. Smaller hotels and bed and breakfasts are scattered throughout the community. And there's the Maranatha Bible Conference Center, a national destination for Christian retreats.

We have broken down pricing into three categories, inexpensive (under $75), moderate ($75 to $150) and expensive ($150 and up). Off-season rates can be 25 to 50 percent below high season rates.

All addresses are within the city of Muskegon unless otherwise noted.

BED AND BREAKFASTS

Port City Victorian Inn

This fully restored 130-year-old house across the street from Muskegon Lake and a short bike ride or drive from the downtown business district offers five historic bedrooms—the Queen Ann Suite, Alexander Rodgers Suite, Captain's Cabin, Rose Room and Anastasia's Room. All rooms include wireless Internet and refrigerators. Breakfast is served in the formal dining room, and tours of this historic property are part of the charm. Moderate to expensive. 1259 Lakeshore Drive. (231) 759-0205 or (800) 274-3574. www.portcityinn. com

White Swan Inn Bed and Breakfast

Within walking distance of Whitehall's specialty shops and restaurants, the White Swan Inn offers four rooms for guests to stay. Choose between the Cygnet Suite, Jasmine Room, Covell Room and Mariner Room. Wireless Internet and DVD players are provided in all bedrooms. Pets can also stay on request. Moderate to expensive. 303 South Mears Avenue, Whitehall. (231) 894-5169 or (888) 948-7926. www.whiteswaninn.com

Cocoa Cottage Bed and Breakfast

Near White Swan Inn and just minutes from Lake Michigan sits the arts and crafts bungalow, Cocoa Cottage Bed and

Breakfast. Surrounded by a beautiful garden, the Hershey Room, Cadbury Room, Godiva Room and the Ghirardelli Suite tempt sweet-toothed guests. The rooms offer wireless Internet, DVD players and plenty of well chosen reading material. Cocoa Cottage is known for its gourmet breakfasts, which have won national awards. The flourless chocolate torte greets you at check-in. Moderate to expensive. 223 South Mears Avenue, Whitehall. (231) 893-0674 or (800) 204-7596. www.cocoacottage.com

A Finch Nest
The 1860 Victorian bed and breakfast offers three well-appointed guest rooms with king- and queen-sized beds. Guests can relax and enjoy spending time near the wood-burning fireplace, in the library, or near the garden. Carrying out the Victorian theme are pedestal sinks and hardwood floors. The bed and breakfast is three blocks from White Lake, walking distance from the Howmet Playhouse and a 20-mile paved bike trail. Moderate. 415 Division Street, Whitehall. (231) 893-5323 or (888) 595-7219. www.afinchnest.com

Village Park Bed and Breakfast
Village Park is a Victorian-style cottage overlooking Pomona Park and Spring Lake with access to Lake Michigan. Choose between the Lakeview Room, Sunrise Room, Sunset Room and the Edgewater Room. Free wireless Internet, complimentary bikes, outdoor hot tub, and hiking trails and beach access at Hoffmaster State Park add to the fun. Moderate. 60 W. Park Street, Fruitport. (616) 502-4628. www.bbonline. com/mi/villagepark

HOTELS

Holiday Inn Muskegon Harbor
In the heart of downtown Muskegon, Holiday Inn is within walking distance of Frauenthal Theater, the Hackley and Hume homes, Hackley Library, the Muskegon Museum of Art and the Muskegon County Museum. The hotel offers executive suites and executive floors, a full service restaurant, a pool and wireless Internet. Moderate to expensive. 939 Third Street. (231) 722-0100 or (800) 846-5253. www. holidayinn.com

Shoreline Inn and Suites
Overlooking Terrace Point on the Lake Michigan shore just two blocks walk from the downtown historic district, this towering 10-story hotel has 140 rooms and suites, including a dozen luxurious penthouse suites that are individually decorated in styles ranging from Victorian to Italian Renaissance to New Orleans style. All guest rooms feature full-sized refrigerators, microwave ovens, coffee makers, cabinets, sinks and ironing boards, as well as Internet data ports, and some have fireplaces. There's a heated indoor pool with two separate whirlpool hot tubs and an exercise room. Breakfast is included. Moderate to expensive. 750 Terrace Point Road. (231) 727-8483 or (866) 727-8488 or (866) 727-8483. www.shorelineinn.com

Weathervane Inn
With a beautiful view of White Lake, guests can stay at the Weathervane Inn and enjoy White Lake's only waterfront

luxury hotel. Twenty-three rooms are available for vacation or business needs. There are also two-room suites and one extended stay apartment. Nineteen rooms have balcony views overlooking the water. The Weathervane Inn also features a conference room, boat docks with Lake Michigan access, and a relaxing hot tub. Breakfast is included. Moderate to expensive. 4527 Dowling Street, Montague. (231) 893-8931 or (877) 893-8931. www.theweathervaneinn.net

MOTELS

Fairfield Inn and Suites
Located across from the Lakes Mall and 15 minutes away from Michigan's Adventure, the Fairfield Inn is nonsmoking and offers free wireless Internet, indoor pool and hot tub, exercise room, complimentary breakfast and a business center. Rooms have coffee makers, lighted desk areas, microwave ovens and refrigerators upon request. Moderate. 1520 Mount Garfield Road, Norton Shores. (231) 799-0100 or (800) 228-2800. www.marriott.com/mkgns

Hampton Inn
Also near the Lakes Mall and the Muskegon Airport, the Hampton Inn offers air-conditioned rooms with Internet access, a fitness center and complimentary breakfast. Microwaves and refrigerators are also available, as are cribs, rollaway beds and connecting bedrooms. There's an indoor pool and whirlpool. Moderate. 1401 East Ellis Road. (231) 799-8333 or (800) 426-7866. www.hampton-inn.com/muskegon

Baymont
The Baymont features free breakfast, high speed Internet, a fitness center and an indoor pool. Other amenities include a whirlpool, sauna, hot tub, meeting rooms and complimentary newspapers in the lobby. Nonsmoking rooms and connecting rooms are also available. The hotel is near the mall and three miles from P.J. Hoffmaster State Park. Moderate. 4677 Harvey. (231) 798-0220 or (800) 434-5800. www.baymontmuskegon.com

IT'S A DOG'S LIFE

Dog lovers find that it's easy to love and leave their animals when they are in Muskegon. Dog Star Ranch is an ideal location to board your pet for a day or longer. Offering three small parks and the spacious 24-acre "canine frontier" with a nature area, two acre ponds and bayou, Dog Star includes training sessions, grooming and a canine rodeo. Overnight boarding ranges from luxury suites to cabin-run camping. Hugs and rubs are available at no extra charge. 4200 Whitehall Road. (866) 766-0444. www.dogstarranch.com

The best place in town for a stroll with your pet, Kruse Park Dog Run begins to the right of the staircase and extends toward Pere Marquette Park. Dogs must be leashed. Kruse Park is located at the west end of Sherman Avenue.

Comfort Inn

Comfort Inn of Muskegon features a private courtyard with patio, indoor and outdoor pools, game rooms, fitness room and a sauna. The inn also offers rooms with whirlpool baths. Services include guest laundry, complimentary breakfast and a business center. Rooms feature microwaves and refrigerators. Wheelchair accessible rooms are available. Moderate to expensive. Right off US 31. 1675 East Sherman Boulevard. (231) 739-9092 or (800) 434-5800. www. comfortinnmuskegon.com

Best Western Inn and Suites

Near Michigan's Adventure, guests can relax after a long day at the park at this 72-room motor inn. Best Western Inn and Suites offers free high-speed Internet, a free continental breakfast, fitness center, indoor pool, Jacuzzi suites, and tennis courts. Moderate. 2822 Durham Road, Whitehall. (231) 893-4833 or (800) 738-8238. www.bestwestern.com

Ramada Inn

The Ramada Inn–Whitehall offers a business-friendly environment. A business center, high speed Internet, meeting and conference rooms and business services such as fax machines, a computer, copy service, overhead projector, and printer make this is a good choice for road warriors. The Ramada Inn also has a fitness center, a courtyard, a game room and an outdoor gazebo picnic and grill area. Moderate. Near Michigan's Adventure. 2865 Colby Road, Whitehall. (231) 893-3030 or (800) 272-6232. www.ramadainnwhitehall.com/virtual

Bel-Aire Motel

This family-owned-and-operated motel is just six minutes from the Muskegon Airport and handy to the Lakes Mall. The motel offers 17 units and is located in a quiet residential area. Wireless Internet access is available in selected rooms, while a microwave or refrigerator is available upon request. Rooms accommodate up to eight people. Inexpensive to moderate. 4240 Airline Road. (231) 733-2196. www.belairemotel.net

Maple Tree Inn

Located in a quiet White Lake neighborhood, the Maple Tree Inn has a good downtown location handy to Lake Michigan. Jacuzzi suites, continental breakfasts, bicycle rentals, wireless Internet and scrapbooking are available. Inexpensive to moderate. 323 South Mears, Whitehall. (231) 894-4091. www.themapletreeinn.com

Montgomery Inn and Suites

Near White Lake's shops, beaches and golf course, the Montgomery Inn and Suites features newly remodeled rooms. The inn offers a child play area and a six-person spa as well as a relaxing front porch. Two-room suites are available with a living room, wet bar, refrigerator, microwave and a fireplace. Wireless Internet. A continental breakfast is provided. Inexpensive to moderate. 10233 US 31, Montague. (231) 894-4339. www.montgomery-inn.com

Montague Mountain Inn

The Montague Mountain Inn offers a continental breakfast, Jacuzzi tubs in all rooms and bicycle and fishing pole rentals. The motel is near a miniature golf course and the popular

Montague Bicycle Trail. Moderate. 9075 Water Street, Montague. (231) 893-4439. www.montague-mountain-inn.com

Pines Motel

Ten minutes from Michigan's Adventure, the Pines Motel is convenient to boat launches, beaches, charter fishing, Putter's Creek miniature golf and go-carts. Inexpensive rooms include microwave and refrigerator. Wireless Internet. 1507 Whitehall Road, North Muskegon. (231) 744-3640. www. mypinesmotel.com

Alpine Motel

Alpine Motel is located close to Muskegon County Airport and the Lakes Mall. Near I-96 and US 31, this establishment is ten minutes from downtown. Wireless Internet. Inexpensive to moderate. 4262 Airline Road. (231) 733-1323. www. alpinemotel.net

Snug Harbor Motel

A budget-priced establishment adjacent to the Muskegon State Park public boat launch, Snug Harbor offers kitchenettes ideal for fisherman. There's a bait and tackle shop on the premises. Inexpensive. 3492 Memorial Drive. (231) 744-3440. www.home.comcast.net/~snugharbormotel

Victory Inn and Suites

This family-friendly four-story motel offers modern, few-frills guest rooms with free wireless Internet access. Facilities include an indoor swimming pool and a sauna. A complimentary continental breakfast is served. Inexpensive. 2967 Henry Street. (231) 733-2651. www.victoryhotelsinter national.com

Causeway Bay Motel

Despite the name, this low-rise motel—the only U.S. location of a Canadian-based chain—is not on Causeway Street; rather, it's just off US 31, a mile from the Lake Michigan shore and six miles from Michigan's Adventure. The standard guest rooms are contemporary and predictable, with free wireless Internet access. The motel also features an indoor pool and hot tub, a fitness room and a game room. Moderate. 150 E. Seaway Drive. (231) 733-4307. www.causewaybayhotels.ca/muskegon.html

RESORTS AND CONFERENCE CENTERS

Michillinda Lodge

On the Lake Michigan shore, historic Michillinda Lodge is a great place for a family retreat, a romantic getaway or an off-season vacation. A short distance from Whitehall and Duck Lake, the lodge offers 52 rooms, group accommodations, a great swimming beach, heated pool, tennis courts, shuffle-board, tennis, basketball and evening events. The lodge restaurant and lounge are popular gathering places. Campfires are a great way to end the day. Complementary breakfast. Wireless Internet. Open year-round, Michillinida features fall and winter bed-and-breakfast deals as well as an off-season couple's special that includes a complimentary bottle of house wine. Moderate to expensive. 5207 Scenic Drive, Whitehall. (231) 893-1895. www.michillindalodge.com

Lakeside Inn

Just minutes from the White River Light Station and Museum and Michigan's Adventure, Lakeside Inn Resort has served White Lake visitors since 1913. Fishing packages include two- and three-bedroom cottages. There's an outdoor swimming pool. Open from April through October, the inn offers lakefront dining through Labor Day. In the winter months, selected cottages are ideal for cross-country skiing and snowmobiling packages. Breakfast included. Moderate to expensive. 5700 North Scenic Drive, Whitehall. (231) 893-8315 or (888) 442-3304. www.lakesideinn.net

Maranatha Conference Center

Maranatha Bible and Missionary Conference Center offers apartments and condominiums in the fall, winter and spring. Located on the Lake Michigan shore, this is a good place for personal retreats. Pastors and their families receive a free night. Some of the country's most highly regarded theologians offer inspirational lectures. Outdoor pool. Wireless Internet. Moderate to expensive. September to May. 4759 Lake Harbor Road. (231) 798-2161. www.vacationwithapurpose.org

DOWNTOWN MUSKEGON

Amid major new development, downtown Muskegon is the place where you sit on the deck of an LST watching *Casablanca* on a warm summer night, enjoy an art fair or a big-name rock concert, see artistic treasures, launch your boat or just read a good book. From symphonic splendor to scenic bike paths, the city's downtown is changing radically. It's even attracted the Michigan Culinary Institute, a sure sign of good restaurants to come.

If you're headed into downtown Muskegon on Interstate 96, don't make the mistake of turning onto US 31. Just keep going. I-96 becomes business US 31 and takes you to the center of town.

A few blocks from the lakeshore, the breezy downtown area is crowded with the oldest and newest buildings in the city, not to mention a wealth of sightseeing opportunities. One can barely walk a block without coming across a park, a garden or an example of regal masonry in castle-like churches and buildings and, of course, the ubiquitous name of Charles Hackley, Muskegon's philanthropist patriarch. Downtown, with its focus on local history, embraces his legacy.

Muskegon's lakes and rivers have always been central to this community's appeal. They were the transportation corridor for the Ottawa and Chippewa Indians, French fur trappers and lumber barons and manufacturers. Muskegon was named by those French trappers exploring the rivers in the 1600s; the name is believed to have been taken from an American Indian phrase meaning "river of marshes." Edward Fitzgerald was the area's earliest known European resident. Arriving in 1748, he so was impressed he never left.

By the 1830s, the lumber industry was gaining steam and had created an economic boom in the Muskegon area. The beautiful historic buildings and homes highlighted here were erected during that era, including the Queen-Anne-style home of Charles Hackley. By the mid-1880s, Muskegon was known as the "Lumber Queen of the World." But by the early part of the 20th century the lumber industry had faded, and Muskegon went into the furniture and automotive parts manufacturing businesses. A mall was ultimately torn down in favor of a traditional pedestrian-oriented downtown.

Today a community-wide effort led by local businesses in partnership with the Muskegon Area Chamber of Commerce, the Muskegon Community Foundation, many civic groups, the city council and the state of Michigan is rebuilding downtown. Breaking news is available at www.downtownmuskegon.org or the Hackley Public Library. Now let's begin our visit to the city's historic downtown:

1. Bear Lake
2. Duck Lake
3. The Lakes Mall
4. Michigan's Adventure
5. Muskegon County Airport
6. Muskegon River
7. Muskegon State Park
8. Mona Lake
9. P.J. Hoffmaster State Park
10. White River

Muskegon County

34

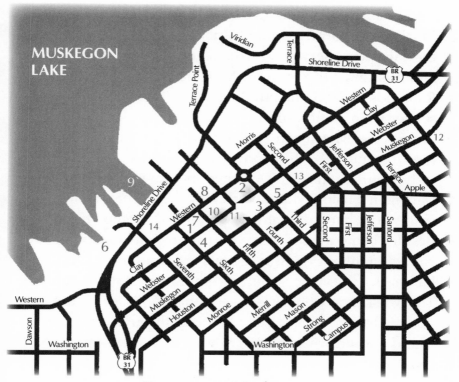

Downtown Muskegon

1. Scolnik House and Fire Barn
2. Frauenthal Theater
3. Hackley Park
4. Hackley and Hume Historic Sites
5. Hackley Public Library
6. Heritage Landing
7. Heritage Memorial Garden
8. L.C. Walker Arena
9. LST 393
10. Monet Garden
11. Muskegon County Museum and Mercantile
12. Muskegon Farmer's Market
13. Muskegon Museum of Art
14. Union Depot / Convention & Visitors Bureau / Trolley Stop

Visitor's Information

Muskegon's former Union Depot on Western Avenue near the lakeshore serves as **Muskegon County Convention and Visitors Bureau**. Built by Chicago & West Michigan Railroads in 1895, the building served as Muskegon's passenger train station until the 1970s, when Amtrak discontinued the Muskegon-Holland train. Vacant throughout the '70s and '80s, the renovated station became the city's visitor bureau in 1995. Designed by Sidney J. Osgood, this Michigan Historic Landmark has the Richardsonian Romanesque charm of many downtown Muskegon buildings. Besides being a good place to pick up information or brochures highlighting Muskegon's cultural and commercial hallmarks, the visitor's bureau is a transportation museum. The Muskegon County Convention and Visitor's Bureau is open 8:00 a.m. to 5:00 p.m. Monday through Friday year-round and on weekends during the summer season. (800) 250-9283. www.visitmuskegon.org

You can pick up a self-guided **audio walking tour** of the downtown area at any of the following locations: Muskegon Area Chamber of Commerce, 900 Third Street; Holiday Inn Muskegon Harbor, 939 Third Street; Hackley Public Library, 316 W. Webster Avenue; or Muskegon County Convention & Visitors Bureau, 610 W. Western Avenue. The tour, which starts in front of the Holiday Inn building at 939 Third Street, is also available for download at www.downtownmuskegon.org

Not up for walking? **The Muskegon Trolley Company** helps you celebrate the moment in style. One trolley or several can transport you and your whole party from one location to another in restored self-propelled comfort. Memorial

Day through Labor Day, the trolley runs a route from downtown to the beach for only 25 cents. (231) 798-1546. Alternatively, the **West Coast Carriage Company** provides horse drawn carriages in the downtown Muskegon area—a great way to explore downtown. 557 West Clay Avenue, Muskegon. (231) 855-2758.

Muskegon's downtown area is also a popular site for regional geocachers who use GPS to locate objects hidden by others. Current hunts can be found at www.geocaching.com.

ART AND CULTURE

A must for any Muskegon visit is the **Muskegon Museum of Art**, just a few blocks from the county museum on Webster Avenue. One of the finest art museums in Michigan, the MMA permanent collection includes John Steuart Curry's classic "Tornado Over Kansas," Edward Hopper's "New York Restaurant" and Winslow Homer's "Answering the Horn." This exceptional museum collection is noteworthy for its turn-of-the-20th-century oil paintings and sculpture, as well as a large collection of 18th and 19th century art. The MMA also represents outstanding local artists in its collection of regional exhibitions and juried shows. Exhibitions showcase famed Midwestern regionalists like Thomas Hart Benton and Grant Wood as well as outstanding children's art, woodcuts and photography. There's also a good gift shop which showcases local artists. At any given time, pieces from their collection may be on loan to great museums around the world. The vast art museum collection, routinely rotated for proper display, is a treasure that draws visitors from around the country. Classes and workshops for all ages teach the basics in a wonderful learning environment. A large juried regional exhibition takes place each summer. Here you'll have a chance to see impressive paintings, glass, sculpture, prints and photography, fiber art and ceramics. Open Tuesday, Wednesday, Friday and Saturday from 10:00 a.m. to 4:30 p.m., Thursday 10:00 a.m. to 8:00 p.m., and Sunday noon to 4:30 p.m. Admission is $4 except on Thursdays, when it is free. Children and youth 17 and under and students with ID receive free admission. 296 W. Webster Avenue. (231) 720-2570. www.muskegonartmuseum.org. A Muskegon Best Bet.

Next door to the Museum of Art, architecture buffs won't want to miss Richardsonian Romanesque **Hackley Public Library**. Built, furnished and stocked with books donated entirely by Charles Hackley, the library opened in 1890 and has been one of the defining fixtures of downtown Muskegon for more than a century. Hackley's only demand for the life of the library was that it would always remain owned by Muskegon County and be open six days a week. Notable features of the library are its stained-glass windows and the opaque white glass floor in the upper stacks. The lovely Julia Hackley Room is a quiet retreat far from the maddening cell phone crowd. The lower level is devoted to genealogical records for patrons seeking information on local bloodlines. The library also has a first-class program for children, along with regular weekly readings and author events. Computer access and free wireless Internet are provided. The library is open Monday through Wednesday 9:00 a.m. to 8:00 p.m., and Thursday through Saturday 9:00 a.m. to 5:00 p.m. (231) 722-7276. www.hackleylibrary.org. A Muskegon Best Bet.

Muskegon County also has an extensive district library system (www.madl.org) as well as a district library serving the White Lake area (www.whitelake.llcoop.org).

Muskegon County Museum & Mercantile, on Clay Street adjacent to Hackley Park, features a large collection devoted to Muskegon's industrial, manufacturing and cultural history. Photographs show Muskegon and the downtown area in its old-time prime. The gallery, a record of early motivations for people who originally came to Muskegon, boasts reconstructions of historical fur traders' cabins, a Great Lakes schooner and a saw mill. The museum's audiovisual displays and a film on the lumbering era add perspective. Downstairs kids will enjoy the wild and intricate world of Great Lakes ecology, with detailed exhibits and dioramas profiling the delicate balance of Muskegon's wetlands, dunes and forests. The Science Room is a special favorite. "Hands-on" is the name of the game here, with pulley systems to manipulate, natural phenomena displays such as a tornado simulator and plenty of other fun for kids of all ages. The Muskegon County Museum is open Monday through Friday, 9:30 a.m. to 4:30 p.m., Saturday and Sunday 12:30 p.m. to 4:30 p.m. Admission is free. 430 W. Clay. (231) 722-0278. www.muskegonmuseum.org. A Muskegon Best Bet.

The Muskegon County Museum of African American History, a recent addition to Muskegon's cultural offerings, is both a focal point of community pride and a resource for education on African American heritage and culture. The museum collects, preserves and interprets memorabilia from the African American experience. The collection sparks children's interest in African American history.

The permanent collection hosts portraits of Martin Luther King, Jr. and Malcolm X. Tuesday through Saturday, 2:30 p.m. to 5:30 p.m. 7 Center Street, Muskegon Heights. (231) 739-9500.

With a railroad library and video collection, model train layouts in three scales, and educational seminars, the **Muskegon Railroad Historical Society** celebrates and maintains Muskegon's rich railroading history. Train lovers won't want to miss it. The historical society also hosts two annual train shows. Tuesday 6:30 p.m. to 9:00 p.m., Saturday 10:00 a.m. to 12:30 p.m. 561 W. Western Avenue. (231) 726-3657. www.mrhs-online.org

Two blocks down Webster Avenue from Hackley Park stand two of the most outstanding examples of Queen Anne architecture in the country: the **Hackley & Hume Historic Sites**. Designed by David S. Hopkins, the houses and their shared carriage barn feature complex 12-tone Victorian paint schemes, multifarious roof levels and intricate chimney construction that perfectly illuminate the glories of the Queen Anne residential style. These buildings have been maintained by the efforts of the Muskegon County Museum and bring the 19th century to life for modern visitors. The two houses on the site, built between 1887 and 1889, were the homes of Charles Hackley, Muskegon's most famous lumber baron and philanthropist, and his business partner, Thomas Hume. Although they were designed by the same architect, the homes are not a matched set. The **Hackley House** has an exotic flair and a wealth of examples of Victorian and late-19th-century decorative arts. Here you'll find Moorish arches suggestive of the Spanish renaissance mixed willy-nilly with exotic Japonesque hand-carved dragons scaling walls and riding down banisters, as well as Greek-inspired carvings of symbolic human faces and lions. The house facades curve up and around these baroque touches, with nary a right angle to be found. The 15 leaded glass windows throughout the house, intricately designed, cast a moody gloom throughout the historic site. The **Hume Home** has a more modern look, with spacious rooms laid out for family life. The walls are adorned with Art Nouveau stencils. The Hackley & Hume Historic Sites are open Wednesday through Sunday from 12:00 noon to 4:00 p.m, May through October, with special hours between Thanksgiving and Christmas. Tours include both houses in succession and cost $3 for visitors 13 and older. (231-722-0278. www.muskegonmuseum.org/hh_site.asp

The stories of families living during the Depression Era are told in the architecture and presentation of the classic Queen Anne-inspired folk Victorian-style **Scolnik House**. This is the only house tour focused specifically on life during the Great Depression era. Museum curators have restored the once crumbling home to portray the furnishings, flooring, appliances and gardens typical of a family living in Muskegon during the late 1920s. The exhibit includes a fictitious Polish Catholic owner and his family and an opportunity to listen in on the party line where you can learn how families "made do." Wednesday through Sunday noon to 4:00 p.m.; May through October. Free admission. 504 West Clay Avenue. (231) 722-0278. www.muskegonmuseum.org/scolnik.asp

The adjacent **Fire Barn Museum** offers a look at Hackley Hose Company Number 2, circa 1875. Kids will love this treasure. Open 12:00 noon to 4:00 p.m. Wednesday to Sunday from May to October. Admission is free. 510 W. Clay. (231) 722-0278. www.muskegonmuseum.org/fb_museum.asp

Another architectural highlight is **The Frauenthal Center for the Performing Arts**, previously the Michigan Theater, one of the few downtown landmarks with no connection to Charles Hackley. The Spanish renaissance structure was built in 1929 by Muskegon showman and movie mogul Paul Shlossman. The theater itself, renovated and modernized, still gleams with colorful and gilded ornamentation typical of the Spanish renaissance, rich velour seats and velvet draperies, cherubs galore and plaster moldings of shells rising to a grand oculus. It is here that the community convenes for concerts, plays, films and musicals by the likes of the West Shore Symphony Orchestra and the Muskegon Civic Theatre. In early February, one can catch the Muskegon Film Festival here, a two-day lineup of independent films made by college students and professional groups from all across the country. The Frauenthal Center is also the home of the Miss Michigan Pageant. (231) 722-9750. www.frauenthal.info

Inside of the Frauenthal Center, located in the lower level lobby, is a local favorite, **City Café**, a bistro with an eclectic menu featuring inventive European and Mediterranean dishes and a distinctive American flair. Despite the elegant menu, dress is casual, making the City Café a wonderful place to meet friends before the show. The wine selection is excellent. Hours are Monday through Thursday, 11:00 a.m. to 8:00 p.m., Friday 11:00 a.m. to 10:00 p.m. and Saturday 5:00 p.m. to 10:00 p.m. Reservations are recommended in order to get a table, since this is one of the finer restaurants in the Muskegon area. (231) 725-7769. www.citycafemuskegon.com

The heart of downtown, **Hackley Park** is the home of Parties in the Park, Friday afternoon/evening benefit summer concerts where you're likely to see bikers, ministers, students, their teachers and a few thousand of your closest friends. At quieter times, it's a great lunchtime idyll. Dedicated by Charles Hackley in 1892, the park has many beautiful examples of turn-of-the-20th-century Civil War memorial sculptures, including Joseph Carabelli's baroque **Soldiers & Sailors Monument**, a 76-foot-tall spire topped with a bronze "Goddess of Liberty." There is also a well preserved collection of four massive stone sculptures of war heroes—Abraham Lincoln, William Glasgow Farragut, Ulysses S. Grant and William Tecumseh Sherman—each standing guard at one of the four corners of the park. The statuary here is a memorable Civil War memorial.

The **Monet Garden of Muskegon**, is a fine pocket garden nestled in the historic downtown area thanks to the support of the City of Muskegon, the Community Foundation and the Master Gardeners. This spot pays homage to the oft-imitated Giverny garden of Claude Monet. Here you'll find foliage framed trellises with gorgeous blooms and a replica of Monet's famous arched bridge over a lily pond. The park is free to the public, a valuable addition to the revitalization and beautification of the downtown area. Clay and Fifth. (231) 724-6361. www.muskegonmaster gardeners.org/monet1.htm

Muskegon's many shorelines have been reclaimed from its lumber and foundry heyday. One of the best is **Heritage Landing,** a sprawling park on the Muskegon Lake waterfront. Once a foundry district, it's now the city's hot spot for entertainment and festivals. At one end is the Paul C. Johnson Pavilion, with a canvas roof resembling the white sails that grace the lake in the summer months. This pavilion is the main stage for many festivals that come to the downtown area, starring headliners like Smokey Robinson and Sammy Hagar. The giant Muskegon Summer Celebration is hosted here, as well the Unity Christian Music Festival and the Michigan Irish Music Festival. A number of these events feature a midway, carnival rides, bright lights, fireworks and food and drink aplenty. Local events are also held here, including community gatherings and ceremonies. From the pavilion, there is a spacious green, often used as spectator picnic seating during main events. Easily accessible by bike or on foot, the park and waterfront areas can also be a quiet retreat. A popular spot for photos is the bridge arching over a Muskegon Lake inlet. Heritage Landing includes a large children's play area. The park is open year-round and is free to the public except during festivals, when entrance fees vary.

Another popular spot is the **Heritage Memorial Garden** on West Western at Fifth Street. A gazebo, fountain and benches make this a good spot to unwind, read a book or enjoy a light lunch al fresco.

Clay Avenue Station, at the corner of Seventh and Clay, was originally the circa 1928 Freres gas station. Saved from demolition in the fall of 2004, the building was relocated and reopened as **Clay Avenue Cellars**, a winery and gallery featuring 30 different local artists. Michigan fruit wines, in a variety of delicious flavors and fruit blends are featured. Wine tasting is offered throughout the year, once or twice a month. Artwork placed throughout the wine shop and crammed upstairs in a more traditional gallery includes watercolors, oil paintings, photographs, pottery, jewelry, sculpture and stained-glass works. In warm weather guests can relax on the porch with a glass of wine or coffee and enjoy the wildflower garden. Clay Avenue Cellars hours vary seasonally. 611 Clay Street. (231) 722-3108. Visit www. clayavenuecellars.com for seasonal information.

Along the waterfront, you'll find three big boats turned tourist attractions—two historical museums and a third vessel that actually leaves the dock for cruises.

LST-393

Walk where heroes have walked! Of the 1,151 LST class ships built during WWII, the LST-393 is one of only two remaining. Guided and self-guided tours are available. Movies are shown on Friday evenings during the summer. Monday through Sunday, 10:00 a.m. to 4:00 p.m., May through September. Adults $5, students $3, children 5 and under free. (231) 730-1477. www.lst393.org

Port City Princess

Don't miss this incredible cruise along sparkling Muskegon Lake and Lake Michigan. View the Lakeshore area from sea. The *Princess* offers lunch, dinner and theme cruises as well as sunset cruises. May through October, sailing from 560 Mart Street in Muskegon. (231) 728-8387. www.portcityprincesscruises.com

SS *Milwaukee Clipper*

The *Clipper* began service in 1904 as a luxury liner carrying passengers throughout the Great Lakes from Buffalo, New York, to Duluth, Minnesota. She was converted to a cross-lake car ferry and made her first voyage from Muskegon to Milwaukee in 1941. Retired in 1970, she served as a museum ship and convention facility at Chicago's Navy Pier and later at Hammond, Indiana. To make room for a casino ship, the *Clipper* was sold in 1997 to the Great Lakes Clipper Preservation Association and returned to Muskegon for the first time in 20 years. The *Clipper*'s normal hours are Memorial Day through Labor Day, 1:00 p.m. to 5:00 p.m. Saturdays and Sundays. Adults $7, Students $5, children under 5 free. However, as this book goes to press, tours are temporarily suspended. Call or check their website for current status. 2098 Lakeshore Drive. (231) 755-0990. www. milwaukeeclipper.com

Great Lakes Naval Memorial and Museum
Here you can take a 90-minute tour of the USS *Silversides*, a World War II submarine, and the USCGC McLane W-146, a Prohibition-era Coast Guard cutter. The *Silversides*, which saw service in the Pacific as part of the naval blockade against Japan, is considered the most decorated WWII submarine still afloat. A maritime museum and gift shop support a number of annual events including the Memorial Day weekend Lost Boat Ceremony, which commemorates the 3,000 submarine crew members who perished in World War II combat. April and October, weekends only, 10:00 a.m to 5:30 p.m.; May and September, weekends 10:00 a.m. to 5:30 p.m. and weekdays 1:00 to 5:30 p.m.; July and August, daily 10:00 a.m. to 5:30 p.m. 1346 Bluff Street. (231) 755-1230. www.glnmm.org

WEST MICHIGAN ARCHITECTURE

The American Institute of Architects has created a handy full-color guide to 40 landmarks in our region. Nine of these treasures are located in the Muskegon area, including the Frauenthal Center for the Performing Arts, the Hackley Public Library, the John and Caroline Torrent House, the Hackley House, Hackley Park and St. Francis de Sales Church. This guide, created with the support of the Frey Foundation, includes the Grand Rapids and Holland areas. Just follow the handy maps and you'll be sure to enjoy landmarks you might otherwise miss. Please note: Although they are not on the AIA map, private homes along Clay and Webster Avenues west of Fourth Street include a number of local landmarks. For more information, contact the AIA at 4090 Lake Drive SE, Grand Rapids, MI 49546. (616) 574-0235. www.aiagv.net

MUSKEGON'S NEW DOWNTOWN

Formerly a working man's town anchored in foundries, lumbering, textiles and furniture, downtown Muskegon is no rust belt. Determined to become a cool city, the downtown area has welcomed developments from Grand Valley State University and Baker College, including the Michigan Culinary Institute set to open in 2009. New developments include multistory retail, residential and office spaces, the ArtWorks artist lofts, waterfront condominiums, a conference center, the rooftop café atop Terrace Plaza, a new furniture store, galleries, restaurants, and beautification projects.

Among the most ambitious of development plans for

downtown Muskegon, **Edison Landing** broke ground in Spring 2008. Developer Dan Henrickson and his company, True North, have lofty visions for the urban "main street," which will trail Lakeshore Drive with a $350-million assortment of two- to three-story retail, office and residential spaces, a multistory hotel complex, a 10-story building anchored by main-floor retail, and a "Green Plan-IT" complex devoted to earth-friendly construction innovations that will feature lodging and "green" retail outlets. Boasting a waterfront boardwalk, this diverse and innovative "Smart Zone" is one of 11 such developments planned throughout the state.

The million-square-foot Shaw Walker furniture complex has been converted into the Watermark residential/commercial and conference center. This tax-free renaissance zone offers Manhattan-style condos with sunny eight-foot-high windows, exposed brick, hardwood floors and classy kitchens, adjacent to Muskegon Lake, the YMCA, marinas, and Heritage Landing. Starting at $94,000, these tax-abated units are a hit with new downtown residents. 930 Washington. (877) 422-2600.

Edison Landing is not the only environmentally minded project to land in Muskegon's new downtown. **The Michigan Alternative and Renewable Energy Center** is placing Michigan on the home front of the green energy movement, serving as a research and education facility built with high-tech and earth-friendly features galore. This demonstration facility features a roof with solar tiles and a windmill, a fuel cell energy storage system, a micro-turbine, pressed-wheat wallboard and flooring made entirely of recycled tires and bamboo. 200 Viridian Drive. The **Annis Water Resources Institute** at The Lake Michigan Center anchors the north side waterfront. This research and development institute serves as one of the world's premier freshwater research centers, surrounded by the waters of Lake Michigan, and berths two research vessels. 740 West Shoreline Drive. Information on both centers can be found at www.gvsu.edu.

Another noteworthy project is the **Michigan Culinary Institute**, with its featured restaurant and bakery. Set to open in 2009, this $11-million, 39,000-square-foot complex will front on Clay Avenue between Second and Third Street. Heading up the program is American Culinary Association master chef Alex Erdmann, who has worked at London's Ritz Hotel.

Amidst all this new development, the city has faithfully preserved landmarks like the **Old Indian Cemetery**, the final resting place for 200 Native Americans. Local Indians began burying their dead here in the mid-18th century. From 1806 to 1854 white settlers were also interred here. Now maintained by the Greater Muskegon Historic Association, the cemetery was deeded to the city by lumber magnate Martin Ryerson. It's located at 298 Morris Avenue, across the street from the post office.

Shopping

Delight the bohemian in you with an eclectic treasure from **Sun Wind and Rain** "lifestyle" boutique. 477 W. Western Avenue. (231) 725-0022. http://www.sunwindandrain.com

Another popular spot is **Jilly's**, an art gallery that has attracted visitors like Michigan's governor, Jennifer Granholm. The place for sand dune hearts, fused glass pieces, chimes and driftwood art, this shop is located at 471 W. Western. (231) 728-1515. www.jillygallery.com

Among the many notable shops that have joined the new downtown is **Hegg's Furniture Gallery**, which has done a fine job of restoring the venerable Century Club. Located at 356 West Western Avenue, this eclectic home design showcase adds a classy note to the downtown commercial landscape. (231) 726-4665. www.heggsfurniture.com. Round out your interior decor with a modern lamp or swanky drapes from **Details and Design**. 563 West Western Avenue, (231) 722-7444.

Hot Rod Harley-Davidson whets the appetite for engines and shine. New and used bikes are available for purchase, and rentals and lessons are offered. Visit Hog Heaven's gift shop for Harley-Davidson-themed accessories, gifts and apparel. 149 Shoreline Drive. (231) 722-3653. www.hotrodhd.com

Revel in a glass of wine and a global assortment of cheeses at **The Cheese Lady**. 197 West Clay Avenue. (231) 728-3000. www.thecheeselady.net

For a complete list of businesses, a printable tourist map and audio walking tour, visit www.downtownmuskegon. org and click on "Visit Downtown."

THE WIRED WORLD

Wireless Internet is available at locations all over Muskegon County. Much of the downtown area is covered by a wide ranging arial zone signal that works in offices, shops, Hackley Park and down by the waterfront. You can pick up a signal at libraries, coffee shops, pizza parlors, restaurants and many other locations. All of the facilities listed below offer unlimited wireless access. If you don't have a laptop, or left yours at home, just stop by a helpful local library where you can access the Internet on their computers. Access time at the library may be limited. Visit www.downtownmuskegon.org/wireless.shtml for more info.

Holiday Inn Muskegon Harbor: 939 Third Street. (231) 722-0100.
Racquets Downtown Grill: 446 West Western Avenue. (231) 726-4007.
Hackley Public Library: 316 West Webster Avenue. (231) 722-7276.
White Lake Community Library: 3900 White Lake Drive, Whitehall. (231) 894-9531.
Muskegon Area District Libraries:
Dalton Branch: 3175 Fifth Street, Twin Lake. (231) 828-4188.
Egelston Branch: 5428 East Apple Avenue. (231) 788-6477.
Fruitport Branch: Park at Third, Fruitport. (231) 865-3461.
Holton Branch: 8776 Holton—Duck Lake Road, Holton. (231) 821-0268.
Montague Branch: 8778 Ferry Street, Montague. (231) 893-2675.
Muskegon Heights Branch: 2808 Sanford Street, Muskegon Heights. (231) 739-6075.
North Muskegon Branch: 1522 Ruddiman, North Muskegon. (231) 744-6080.
North Shores Branch: 705 Seminole Road. (231) 780-8844.
Ravenna Branch: 12278 Stafford, Ravenna. (231) 853-6975.

MUSKEGON'S GREAT OUTDOORS

Dense woods and lush fields, rolling farmlands and varied orchards, lakes and rivers—Muskegon's great outdoors is packed with great scenery. Whether you are hiking a trail or camped out at a state park, you will come to love the beauty of this area. This chapter guides you through camping and beaches, Michigan's famous color tours, and a variety of fun and relaxing outdoor sites for the whole family to enjoy.

CITY PARKS

City parks are maintained by the City of Muskegon Leisure Services. Pavilions at the parks can be reserved by calling (231) 724-6704.

Beachwood Park

Beachwood Park offers winter and summer fun for everyone in the family. The park pavilion allows families to warm up in the wintertime or cookout with family and friends during the summer. Kids can enjoy the playground, which includes slides, monkey bars and tire swings. A basketball court is also available. In the winter season, families enjoy using the sledding hills and fire pit. Visitors can also walk, bike or just drive to Pere Marquette Beach by following the boardwalk. Beach Street at Resort Street. www.muskegon-mi.gov/community/parks

Seyferth Park

Just off of Sherman Drive, Seyferth is a well-rounded family park convenient to two ice cream stands, Frosty Oasis and Fat Jack's, as well as Lake Michigan. Teens and children interested in skateboarding and in-line skating enjoy Seyferth's skating facilities as many parents look on. The skate park was built in 1999 and has 13 ramps. There is also a play area for younger kids, as well as a soccer and football fields. Basketball courts and a hockey rink are also available. Sport practices are frequently held here. W. Sherman between Leon and LeBouf. www.muskegon-mi.gov/community/parks

Lake Harbor Park

With 4,000 feet of Lake Michigan frontage, 2,000 feet on the Mona Lake Channel and an additional frontage on Mona Lake, this is one of the city's best retreats. Come for an hour or stay for the day. This 180-acre park at the Lake Harbor Bridge features hiking and cycling paths, fishing, great sunsets, picnic facilities and grills. Dunes, wooded terrain and great vantage points on two lakes make Lake Harbor a best bet for visitors of all ages. A relaxing place ideal for unwinding, beachcombing and photography, this is one of the community's hidden gems. There is no lifeguard. 4635 Lake Harbor Road, Norton Shores. (231) 799-6802. www.nortonshores.org

Ross Park

Located on Mona Lake's south shore, this 43-acre park with over 400 picnic tables is a popular spot for swimming, boating and water skiing. A "tot lot," a pair of inline hockey rinks, a volleyball court, three slow-pitch softball fields, a nine-post Frisbee golf course, horseshoe courts and tennis courts with lights that can be activated until 10:00 p.m. make this one of the community's favorite day-use parks. It is also home to the annual Ross Park Art Fair in August. There is no lifeguard. 1211 Randall Road, Norton Shores. (231) 799-6802. www.nortonshores.org

Mona Lake Park

Convenient to Seaway Drive, this fine lakeshore picnic spot has a large children's play area, change facilities and a launch ramp handy for boats, canoes and kayaks. Soccer and baseball fields, a basketball court, bike and walking paths add to the fun. Lakeshore Boulevard and Holt Street off Seaway Drive (Business US 31), Muskegon Heights.

McGraft Park

On Ruddiman Creek, just a block from Muskegon Lake, McGraft Park is busy year-round. Tennis and basketball courts, shuffleboard, a disc golf course, a baseball field, a horseshoe pit, cross-country skiing, a sledding hill and a play area attract kids from five to 105. An open-air amphitheatre hosts concerts on warm summer nights. The community building is a popular gathering spot for reunions and picnics. To make reservations, call the Department of Leisure Services at (231) 724-6704. Glen Avenue at Wickham. www.muskegon-mi.gov/community/parks

Kruse Park
If you're planning a beach gathering, this park named for a former Muskegon mayor is worth considering. Its pavilion and beach areas can accommodate you and several hundred of your closest friends. Kruse Park has three shelters with electric outlets and barbeque grills as well as picnic tables that seat 50 to 200 people. The park offers direct access to Bronson Beach, a quiet alternative to Pere Marquette. The north end of the beach features a popular dog run. The scenic overlook is a great spot to capture the sunset. Visitors can walk around on steps that weave in the sand dunes and surrounding woods. The park also offers a basketball court and large play area. To make reservations, contact Muskegon's Department of Leisure Services at (231) 724-6704. End of Sherman Boulevard at Beach Street. www.muskegon-mi. gov/community/parks

Pere Marquette Park
This beach offers 27.5 acres of public sandy beach, perfect for relaxing, swimming, volleyball and sand castle construction. There is a large play area for children, picnic tables, changing facilities and snack bar. Captain Jacks offers

live entertainment on weekends. Dockers Fishhouse and Lounge, located in the nearby subdivision, is also a popular spot for weekend music. Fishing off the channel breakwater is always popular. A 200-foot walkway offers wheelchair access to the beach. Visitors should pay attention to the flag warning system when waves are high. We advise staying out of the water in stormy or high wave conditions, particularly when there are no lifeguards. Pay close attention to children going in the water here and proceed with caution on the breakwater. 1601 Beach Street. www.muskegon-mi.gov/community/parks

Margaret Drake Elliot Park

Margaret Drake Elliot, the distinguished nature writer and author, was one of the nation's first woman journalists covering the outdoor beat for a daily paper, the *Muskegon Chronicle*. A teacher and naturalist, Elliot also wrote environmental books. The park named in her honor offers a big playground, picnic tables, a pavilion and a path along the Muskegon Lake Channel. The park is located next to the USS *Silversides* submarine. On Lake Street adjacent to Pere Marquette Park.

STATE AND COUNTY PARKS AND BEACHES

PJ Hoffmaster State Park

This 1,200-acre state park, one of Michigan's best, features three miles of sandy Lake Michigan beaches and 293 campsites. Each site has water and electrical hookups. Reservations are always a good idea during the summer season, as this family-friendly campground fills up early. Hoffmaster features 10 miles of hiking trails, notably, the Dune Climb Stairway, a set of steps leading to the top of a high sand dune and an observation deck that offers a panoramic view of Lake Michigan. The picnic and day use area is perfect for beachcombers. Excellent cross-country trails are popular in the winter months but first check with the Gillette Visitor Center office or park headquarters before proceeding. Some of the hilly trails require intermediate level experience and should be avoided by beginners. Don't miss the Trillium Festival. As at all state parks in the area, a parking pass is required for day use. A daily parking pass costs $6 for Michigan residents, $8 for nonresidents; an annual pass costs $24 for residents, $29 for nonresidents.

The Gillette Center features exhibits on the area's rich dune history, as well as flora and fauna. Between Memorial Day and Labor Day, stop in Tuesday through Saturday between 10:00 a.m. and 5:00 p.m. and Sunday from 12:00 noon to 5:00 p.m. Between Labor Day and Memorial Day, the Center is open Tuesday through Friday from 12:00 noon to 4:00 p.m. and Saturday from 10:00 a.m. to 4:00 p.m. Campground reservations can be made well in advance by calling (800) 447-2757. www.midnrreservations.com/campgrounds. A Muskegon Best Bet.

Muskegon State Park

This 165-acre, 253-site camping area with two separate campgrounds is an ideal vacation spot. The campgrounds are located on the shores of Lake Michigan and Muskegon Lake, with 106 campsites at the Lake Michigan campground and 147 campsites at the South Channel campground. You'll have a hard time finding better beaches and dunes and the price is definitely right.

Offering two miles of Big Lake frontage, the woodsy Lake Michigan campground offers fine hiking trails as well as easy access to Ruth Ann's Ice Cream Stand, a local favorite. At the South Channel location, you will be able to watch freighters and pleasure boats pass through the Muskegon Channel. This handy location gives easy access to both Lake Michigan and the Muskegon Lake shoreline. Close by are the dune hiking trails of Snug Harbor. The Muskegon Lake shore is a popular spot for day trippers who drop anchor and wade ashore. Because of the boat traffic, expect this campsite to be noisier than the Lake Michigan site. It is also has less shade that the main campground to the north.

Among the popular hiking trips are the three-quarter-mile trek to Lost Lake and the five-mile Loop-to-Loop Trail. The park is ideal for biking, and the Winter Sports Complex is a popular spot for skiing, skating and sliding down the luge track (now also open in the summer months). A parking pass is required for day use.

To make reservations at Muskegon State Park, call (800) 447-2757 or visit the website at www.midnrreservations. com/campgrounds. A Muskegon Best Bet.

Pioneer County Park
This 145-acre county park on Scenic Drive, north of Muskegon, is on Lake Michigan and open year-round. The campground has 235 sites, shaded and open, with electrical and water hookups. The campground at Pioneer also features overlook decks and a 2,000-foot-long Lake Michigan beach.

Besides camping, Pioneer County Park also offers picnicking, swimming, sunbathing, tennis, softball, basketball and volleyball. The park is also conveniently located close to Michigan's Adventure amusement park.

Reservations are not available at Muskegon County parks. Arrive at the park early in the morning or afternoon on the day you plan to check in. A $4 Muskegon County Parks vehicle permit or $20 annual pass is required. For more information, call the Muskegon County Parks and Recreation Office at (231) 744-3580.

Meinert County Park
This hidden treasure of a county park is known for its rolling dunes, scenic overlooks and unimproved trails. Spread over 88 acres, the park has excellent views of Lake Michigan and Little Flower Creek, as well as the surrounding countryside. The 67 campsites at Meinert County Park have electrical and water hookups. Meinert County Park is open daily year-round. A parking pass is required for day use.

Reservations are not available at Muskegon Country parks. Arrive at the park early in the morning or afternoon on the day you plan to check in, as campsites fill up early in the summer season. Call the parks office at (231) 744-3580 or contact Meinert Park directly at (231) 894-4881.

Blue Lake County Park
This inland campground features 25 sites on beautiful Big Blue Lake, perfect for fishing, picnicking and water-skiing. Each of the sites has electrical and water hookups and is within walking distance of public restrooms. Quiet and secluded, the Blue Lake County Park offers a getaway from

the crowds along Lake Michigan during the summer. A parking pass is required for day use.

Blue Lake County Park's campsites are first-come, first-served. Arrive at the campground early on the day you plan to check in. Call the Muskegon Country Parks and Recreation Office at (231) 744-3580, or contact Blue Lake Park directly at (231) 894-5574. This is a seasonal number and may not be available during the off-season.

Duck Lake State Park

An ideal day-use family facility with beaches on both Lake Michigan and Duck Lake, this is a great spot for picnicking, hiking, dune climbing, fishing, small boating and, in the winter, cross-country skiing. A channel linking Duck Lake to Lake Michigan is also a popular spot for children and their parents. This is one of Muskegon County's best bets, a short drive north of Muskegon State Park and five miles south of Whitehall and its lighthouse museum. With meadows, hardwood forests and sandy beaches, Duck Lake is a local favorite. Even when Lake Michigan water temperatures are on the chilly side, Duck Lake can be warmer and inviting. Don't make the mistake of parking on busy Scenic Drive along the Lake Michigan shore. Be sure to turn into the State Park parking lot (just north of the bridge) where there is safer parking and easy access to the inland and Big Lake beaches. 3560 Memorial Drive, North Muskegon. (231) 744-3480.

ADDITIONAL CAMPING

Fisherman's Landing

Located on the east end of downtown, Fisherman's Landing offers boat launch ramps, fish cleaning stations, picnic areas and playgrounds. Seventy campsites offer electrical and water hookups. The campsite is pet friendly. Reservations are recommended. (231) 726-6100.

White River Campground

White River Campground is large, with 235 sites, most of them equipped with electrical and water hookups. The campground also offers a handful of cabins with a two-night minimum.

This modern, family-friendly campground is popular with kayakers and canoers because of the easy access it provides to the popular White River. You can rent boats upstream at Happy Mohawk. Onsite activities include an in-ground heated pool, a playground, basketball and volleyball courts, horseshoe pits, and rental areas for canoes, kayaks and tubes. New to the park in 2008 is free wireless Internet. (231) 894-4708. www.whiterivercampground.com

Lake Sch-Nepp-A-Ho

Although it's located adjacent to busy US 31, Lake Sch-Nepp-A-Ho is convenient for travelers headed to Michigan's Adventure and other popular attractions. Offering cabins—some with air conditioning—and campsites, this family-oriented spot has a recreation hall and welcomes pets on leash. 3901 East Tyler Road at US 31. (231) 766-2209. www.michigan-campgrounds,com

KOA of Muskegon

Located off US 31 north of M-12, KOA Muskegon has two private lakes, swimming, fishing, pedal boating and kayaking. It'a also handy to Michigan's Adventure. Choose between wooded and open areas. 3500 Strand. (800) 562-3902 or (231) 766-3902. www.koa.com / where / mi / 22106

Oak Knoll Family Campground

Located 12 miles east of Lake Michigan, Oak Knoll is handy to the White Lake and Fremont areas, about 20 minutes north of Muskegon. Family-oriented, Oak Knoll has tetherball, basketball and volleyball, plenty of shaded sites and easy access to Big Blue Lake, where you can fish, water-ski or kayak. Pets are welcome. 1522 Fruitvale Road, Holton. (231) 894-6063. www.oakknollfamilycampground.com

Other nearby campgrounds include **Bob Ely's Kountry Kamping** (231-853-2029); **Cross-n-Creek Campground** (231-853-5343, www.cross-n-creek.com); **Lake Fran Campground** (231-670-5251); **Trailway Campground** (231-894-4093); **Wolf Lake Resort and Campground** (231-788-4129); and **Muskegon Elks Lodge 274 Park** (231-798-1574).

SCENIC TRIPS

Muskegon Fall Color Tours

Muskegon's Depot-to-Depot Tour is a great way to drive or bike during the fall color season. Along the way you can enjoy coastal views, woodlands and the region's famous dunes. There are many fine photo opportunities, and this less traveled fall route is among the finest of fall escapes. You can visit art museums, historic homes, the world's largest weathervane in Montague and the White River Nature Trail next to the chamber of commerce office. Stop at one of the dozens of attractions along the way, or venture off the beaten path a little and see what you can find; we bet it will be pasty huts, u-pick farms or quaint markets and restaurants.

- Begin in Muskegon's historic Lakeshore District, where a bike path (or Lakeshore Drive) will take you along Muskegon Lake to the downtown business district.
- Stop at Historic Union Depot, now home of the local visitor's bureau at 610 West Western for downtown tour tips.
- At the Hackley Library you can borrow an MP3 player for a self guided tour of historic and architectural landmarks.
- From downtown, continue via bike path (or drive) across the Muskegon River Causeway to North Muskegon.
- Turn left at Lake Avenue and follow it out along Scenic Drive, past the dunes of Snug Harbor to Muskegon State Park.
- Continue north past Duck Lake to the White River Light Station Museum.
- Head back east on South Shore Drive into Whitehall, Business 31 and the White Lake Depot.

By bike this is a full-day trip. By car allow at least five hours with stops. For detailed directions, check with the

White Lake Chamber of Commerce at www.whitelake.org or the Muskegon Visitor's Bureau. (231) 724-3100.

Every October, the community gathers to hike or bike the trails together from Muskegon to White Lake during fall color season. Several designated scenic and historical sites are mapped into this depot-to-depot tour. A $5 entry fee includes free passes to Hackley & Hume Historic Site, Great Lakes Naval Memorial and Museum and White River Light Station and Museum.

OUTDOOR RECREATION

Winter Sports Complex

Muskegon's Winter Sports Complex, which includes the luge training ground where Olympic 2002 Silver and 1998 Bronze Medalist Mark Grimette practiced, is not just for pros. It's also a great facility for anyone who wants to ice skate, ski or enjoy Michigan's only public luge course. Located in Muskegon State Park, this recreational center is perfect for the whole family. Lighted cross-country ski tracks make this a perfect outing on a starry winter night. During the daytime you're likely to spot deer or wild turkey. There is also an ice skating trail through the woods. A ski and skate shop, moderate prices and a snack bar give visitors a chance to try several sports on the same outing. A cozy lodge is perfect for warming up between activities. A wheeled luge program for summer visitors is also offered. 462 Scenic Drive. (231) 744-9629. www.msports.org

HIKING AND BIKING TRAILS

Lakeshore Trail
This paved biking trail provides photogenic views of Lake Michigan, Muskegon Lake, and a variety of local parks and natural attractions. Construction is under way for trail expansions planned in three sections. The trail also leads into downtown Muskegon where you can stop for a bite to eat. The trail begins at the causeway and can also be accessed from numerous points along the lakeshore such as McCracken Avenue. For a map of the route, go to www.visitmuskegon.org/trails.

Musketawa Trail
This 26-mile trek winds through river bottoms, farmlands and small towns. The wheelchair-accessible trail is open to bikers, snowmobilers, horseback riders, inline skaters, cross-country skiers, hikers and nature lovers. Take US 31 to Sherman Boulevard East, then turn left on Broadway. The parking area for the trailhead is one mile down Broadway. For a complete map and additional access information, head to www.visitmuskegon.com/trails.htm or view the trail's website at www.musketawatrail.org. (231) 821-0553.

Hart-Montague Trail State Park
For an hour or a day, any part of this 22.5-mile journey is a great way to enjoy a west Michigan highlight. Available to hikers, bikers, cross-country skiers and snowmobilers, this route takes you along scenic byways through farmland, forests and small towns. Horseback riding is only permitted on asphalt sections of the route. Wheel-

chair accessible. The northern trailhead is located at John Gurney Park in the city of Hart. The south trailhead sits at the White Lake Community Library. Restrooms, ice cream parlors and other amenities are available along the trail. Visit www.visitmuskegon.com/trails.htm for a trail map or head to www.whitelake.org/bike.html for more information. A Muskegon Best Bet.

WINDSURFING, KITEBOATING, SURFING AND KITE FLYING

The documentary *Unsalted* offers an intriguing look at surfing the Great Lakes. Although the area is more suited to the boogie board, Lake Michigan waves in the spring and fall can be awesome for surfing. Naturally the chilly waters demand a wetsuit. Perhaps a safer and more reliable bet is windsurfing or kite surfing, two popular lakefront activities. Kite flying is also hard to beat along Lake Michigan. Check out MacKite at www.mackiteboarding.com/muskegon.htm for handy tips on kiteboarding local waters. You must stay away from the swimming areas and, of course, at all times avoid the breakwalls and the water filtration plant near the south end of Pere Marquette Beach.

Mackinaw Kites and Toys at Pere Marquette Beach (in season only) and in nearby Grand Haven is the place to go for kiteboarding and kite supplies. They offer a two-day deluxe kiteboarding training camp and lessons. (616) 846-7501 or (800) 622-4655. www.mackite.com/home.htm

OFF-ROAD VEHICLES, MOTORCYCLES AND CROSS-COUNTRY SKIING

Musketawa and Hart-Montague Trails, Duck Lake State Park, Muskegon State Park, Hoffmaster State Park and the Muskegon Winter Sports Complex all offer trails and snow-play areas for cross-country skiing.

Cedar Creek Motorsport Trail

Wind through the incredible Huron-Manistee National Forest, a true Michigan gem. Department of Natural Resources-licensed off-road vehicles can operate on designated roads and trails. Vehicles must be less than 50 feet wide on motorized trails. The two-way, 24-mile track is closed unless posted *Open*. Located in northeast Muskegon County, between Holton and Twin Lake. Parking is just south of Ryerson Road on Linderman Road. Trail information is available on a bulletin board in the lot. (800) 821-6263.

Horseshoe and Holton Motorcycle Trails

This 58-mile motorcycle-only track is located in the Huron-Manistee National Forest. A Michigan Secretary of State street-legal license is required in addition to DNR ORV licensure. Trails are located in the southeast portion of Oceana County and the northeast portion of Muskegon County. Trails fall within 10 miles of Fremont, Hesperia and Holton. Parking at intersection of McKinley and 184th Avenue and on Brunswick Road east of Blue Lake Road. Closed unless posted *Open*.

CANOEING AND KAYAKING

Don't miss a chance to explore the backcountry by easily navigable rivers. Some of the best canoeing, kayaking and rafting in Michigan is found on the state's longest river, the Muskegon. This river, framed by vast stands of oak, pine, beech and maple, is a great place to spot deer and turtles. You may also see an occasional bald eagle. Beginning at its headwaters near Houghton Lake, the Muskegon is, according to author Jeff Alexander, "one of the largest rivers in the Great Lakes Basin. Its watershed, which spans 2,724 square miles, accounts for 5 percent of the Lake Michigan drainage basin and spans an area larger than the state of Delaware." In his book *The Muskegon: The Majesty and Tragedy of Michigan's Rarest River*, Alexander, who also writes for the *Muskegon Chronicle*, tells the story of this scenic river, which also has some of the best fishing in the state. After reading Alexander's book, you'll surely want to explore the Muskegon for yourself.

High bluffs known as "rollaways" were perfect for sending fresh cut pine logs down to the river banks, where the timber was dispatched to Muskegon's flourishing lumber mills, which provided materials to rebuild Chicago after the Great Fire of 1871. Today the same area is a recreational center. A good place to discover the charms of this 170-mile-long river is the Croton Dam/Newaygo area. Although this region with its public and private campgrounds can be very busy on summer weekends, much of the year it is blissfully uncrowded, particularly on spring and fall weekdays.

All or part of the forested 13-mile journey from Croton Dam to Newaygo is a memorable journey. Broad, winding stretches are a perfect retreat on a hot day. While there are many homes and cottages in the area, there are still plenty of secluded spots and pools ideal for a dip. Longer journeys leading another 14 miles to Bridgeton and ultimately to Muskegon Lake are available for overnight travelers. Be forewarned, the river, with three branches, is fast-moving in spots, and you may want to brush up on your paddling technique before setting out or else settle for a less adventurous float trip. If you're thinking of a longer trip, plan carefully. No need to panic; just be sure to wear a lifejacket and listen carefully to instructions from the marinas that deliver you and your canoe or kayak to the river bank.

One of the great things about the Muskegon River is that, except in the dead of winter, it is navigable almost year-round. There is good salmon fishing in October and excellent steelheading in March and April. One outfitter that prides itself on service in- and off-season is Newaygo's **Wisner Canoe Rental**, just off the Highway 37 bridge. An hour northeast of Muskegon, this establishment provides fishing boats, canoes and kayaks, although you must make reservations in the off season. They also offer car spotting service. 25 Water Street, Newaygo. (231) 652-6743. Another popular outfitter is **Croton Dam Float Trips**, 5355 Croton Road, Newaygo, (231) 652-6037. It's always a good idea to call ahead before setting out for a day-long trip. A Muskegon Best Bet.

You can rent a canoe, kayak or tube at **Happy Mohawk Canoe Livery** on the White River. Call ahead. 735 Fruitvale Road, Montague. (231) 894-4209. Another good place is **Powers Outdoors**, which both rents and sells canoes. 4523 Dowling Street, Montague. (231) 893-0687. www.powersoutdoors.com. You'll also find canoes for rent at **River**

Rat Canoe Rentals, 8702 River Drive, Grant. (231) 834-9411. www.riverratcanoerental.com

BIRDING

Birders from around the state and across the country flock to Muskegon for good reason. This region offers some of the best bird watching in Michigan: a wide variety of easily accessible marshlands, river bottoms, shoreline and wooded areas. If you've never been a birder, this is the place to start. Please pay special attention to the following guidelines for a safe, pleasurable experience. It is always a good idea to wear safe reflective clothing when out birding. For your safety we also strongly recommend bird-watching with a companion and carrying a cell phone.

A good choice for birdwatchers eager to get the jump on the best vantage points in town is **The Nuthatch**, where you'll find excellent local guides along with staff suggestions that will add to your viewing pleasure. 2320 Sherman Boulevard, Muskegon. (231) 759-3303.

The **Muskegon County Nature Club**, a chapter of the Michigan Audubon Society, provides monthly field trips ideal for fledgling birdwatchers. For a complete schedule, locator map and more information, go to the club's website (members.tm.net/mcnc) or contact President Diane Morton-Pletcher at (231) 740-6910 or Audubon Representative Ric Pedler at (231) 739-7000.

Here is the club's top-down list of 13 excellent birding sites in Muskegon County compiled by Brian Johnson:

1. *Lane's Landing:* On a good weather day birders can see or hear over 100 species here during the peak of the spring migration. West off Maple Island Road one mile north of the Muskegon Wastewater entrance.

2. *The Muskegon Wastewater System:* Lagoons, dikes and fields east of Maple Island Road and north of Apple Avenue (M-46) attract migrating shorebirds, waterbirds and raptors. Grass fields south of Apple Avenue are excellent for upland sandpiper, short-eared owl, sparrows and hawks. Known throughout the state, this area is patrolled by a sheriff's deputy. You must register with the office and receive a pass to watch birds here. Please consult the box on pages 78–79 for details.

3. *Muskegon State Park:* This park provides excellent birding with paths leading south to the Muskegon Channel and north around Lost Lake. Dunes north of the Muskegon Channel provide good viewing of migrating hawks. A State Park sticker is required. Snug Harbor on Ruddiman Drive west of North Muskegon.

4. *Causeway Area:* View birds along the sidewalks of Veterans Memorial Park. Look for breeding peregrine falcons on the B.C. Cobb Plant smokestack. Songbirds abound in the thick habitat of the Muskegon Lake Nature Preserve northwest of the causeway. View waterbirds from the birdwatching sign on the Muskegon Conservation Club property west of the preserve. East end of Muskegon Lake between Muskegon and North Muskegon.

5. *Muskegon State Game Area Headquarters:* The loop path along the banks of the Maple River and adjacent woods and fields provide nearly as many species as Lane's Landing. Excellent for spring warblers, resident trumpeter swans, and black-billed and yellow-billed cuckoos. Adjacent to Lane's Landing, accessible from Maple Island Road a mile north of the Lane's Landing entrance.

6. *Pere Marquette Park*: Check the breakwater rocks at "The Ovals" city park on the shore of Lake Michigan south of the Muskegon Channel for purple sandpipers from late fall through winter when conditions are safe. Look along the lakeshore anytime for gulls, water birds and raptors. Also try along the one-mile channel wall and at Kruse Park, two miles south at the end of Sherman Boulevard.

7. *White River Marsh:* View birds from the walking path along the east side of Business US 31 between Whitehall and Montague. During migration raptors cruise the flats. Waterfowl are common in the open water. The cattail stands harbor typical marsh species like herons, rails and swallows.

8. *Hoffmaster State Park:* This combination of woodland, stream, dune and shoreline habitats provides very good birding in the breeding season and during migrations. A State Park sticker is required. Between Grand Haven and Muskegon at the west end of Pontaluna Road.

9. *White Lake Channel:* Like the Muskegon Channel on a smaller scale. Duck species such as bufflehead, common goldeneye, greater and lesser scaup and redhead can be

seen when the lakes start to freeze. For whatever reason, this channel is more reliable for long-tailed ducks and scoters. Grebes also occur here. West of the White Lake Country Club.

10. *Lake Harbor Park and Mona Lake Channel:* Lake Harbor Park is mostly a migrant songbird site. Although small, its proximity to Lake Michigan can supply good diversity and numbers. In the winter the boardwalk offers views of waterfowl and gulls. These birds may be far out or just off the channel. North side of the channel west of Lake Harbor Road.

11. *Ravenna Sewage Ponds:* Southwest of the village of Ravenna, this migrant waterfowl and shorebird site is like the Muskegon Wastewater System on a much smaller scale.

12. *Hilton Park Road:* Excellent for spring migrants. During breeding season, regularly-occurring birds include Acadian flycatcher and great horned owl. Unfortunately, the smell of dead fish is often present here. One mile west of the Wastewater properties at the road's northern end.

13. *Mill Iron Road:* Bird feeders on private property, but viewable from the public access site where the road ends at the Muskegon River, provide every possible feeder bird in wintertime, including all six local woodpecker species. The power line easement a quarter mile south of the dead-end provides excellent birding west to the river during spring migration and the breeding season. Midway between Muskegon and the Wastewater properties.

MUSKEGON WASTEWATER
BIRDING INFORMATION

The state-of-the-art Muskegon Wastewater Management System, encompassing 11,000 acres, includes aeration and settling basins, storage lagoons and irrigated croplands. This purification system, which sends clean water back into the Muskegon River and Black Creek, is so vast that it can be spotted by astronauts orbiting the earth. Birders are welcome as long as they are registered and carry the required daily or yearly pass, available weekdays at the headquarters office located at 8301 White Road. (231) 724-3440. Be sure to ask about any special driving or weather restrictions before heading out.

Safety Note: There is truck traffic in the area, which means you should always stand well off the roadway when birdwatching. Be sure to wear reflective clothing. For your safety, don't even think about exploring this area in low visibility situations, particularly heavy fog and icy winter weather. Once on the dikes, simply use common sense. When stopping, pull off to the side to allow wastewater trucks or other vehicles to drive past. Driving here after dusk is out of the question. Be on your way before sunset.

To access the public entrance, take Apple Avenue east from Muskegon to Maple Island Road, turn left and head north three miles. From here turn right into the entrance and head east about a mile, checking any small lagoons to your right that might have water in them plus the pylons along your left where raptors roost. Then turn right (south) to the headquarters building parking lot. After picking up your pass at the office, drive up onto the dikes. You'll be near the south end of the main dike separating the two large lagoons.

There is also an entrance on Swanson Road just north of Apple Avenue, immediately north of the landfill (don't go into the landfill driveway). You'll be at the southeast corner of the large east lagoon.

There's also good birding on the Wastewater properties south of Apple Avenue. Drive south from Apple on Swanson Road one mile to Laketon (unmarked intersection) where there's a model airplane airport. In season, these grasslands support many sparrow species along with ring-necked pheasant, bobolink, upland sandpiper, Brewer's blackbird, dickcissel and short-eared owl.

If you continue another quarter mile south on Swanson from Laketon you'll drive through a tiny marsh and find an abandoned orchard on your left as well as a small pond to your right. All these areas are good for birding.

Also try birding west of the Swanson-Laketon intersection. Depending on season and habitat you might see orchard oriole, northern mockingbird or northern shrike. The unmarked two-track (Seba Road) one half mile west of Swanson on Laketon is usually passable to the north as far as a small stand of trees where many bird species may be found. Be sure to proceed with caution and turn back if the road is in poor condition. Check at headquarters before exploring this area.

DIVERSITY IN NATURE

The Muskegon area has a great diversity of habitat types. It is blessed with open dunes, wooded backdunes, coastal plain marshes, interdunal wetlands, several forest types and one of the state's largest river systems, the Muskegon River corridor and related tributaries. Muskegon, the midway point on the lower peninsula, is often referred to as Michigan's climatic tension zone. Cooler summers and lower evaporation rates are typical of the peninsula's northern region, while warmer summers and higher evaporation are typical to the south. This climatic tension zone, which runs from Muskegon to Bay City, also influences animal and plant populations. Here you can often find species native to the south or to more northern areas. For instance, around Muskegon one might see both northern, *(Glaucomys sabrinas)*, and southern, *(Glaucomys volans)* flying squirrels.

Lake Michigan and the area's bountiful natural resources add tremendously to Muskegon's quality of life. The big lake also has a moderating effect on the region's climate, resulting in warmer fall months and a somewhat later arrival of spring than what occurs at similar latitudes farther inland. The lake can influence more than seasonal temperatures. Many microclimates exist along the lakeshore and its sand dunes, allowing for the emergence and success of plant species normally found growing in more southern locations. This is also true of nesting birds. The protected shoreline areas buffered by towering sand dunes, sheltered backdune forests and other unique habitats are a seasonal home for such songbirds as hooded, prairie, cerulean and prothonotary warblers. Muskegon's public natural areas and parks are critical habitat to the wildlife and plant species that university students and professors from throughout Michigan have tracked and monitored for over a hundred years, thoroughly documenting Muskegon's rich botanical and wildlife heritage and how it adds to the aesthetic, recreational and educational value of the community. To learn more about specific plants and animals to look for when visiting Muskegon we recommend you read *A Number of Things: A Year of Nature* by Muskegon naturalist and longtime *Muskegon Chronicle* writer Margaret Drake Elliott. You will be amazed by all Muskegon has to offer in the way of a natural experience.

SPORTS AND RECREATION

MUSKEGON LOCAL SPORTS

Any given Friday night in the fall is a bad time for telemarketing in Muskegon. Much of the town is out cheering on their favorite team. By the time they get home, many have lost their voices. As you would expect in a region famous for football champions, Muskegon takes prep sports seriously. The Muskegon Big Reds have one of the best programs in the nation and regularly send stars off to major teams ranging from the University of Michigan to the University of Southern California. In addition Muskegon Heights has a strong basketball tradition, too, and West Michigan Christian regularly wins state soccer titles. There's a strong women's sports program at many local high schools, as well.

Ice hockey has been a tradition in Muskegon since 1960, when the Muskegon Zephyrs began playing at the L.C.

Walker Arena. After winning a Turner Cup championship in 1962, the team was renamed the Muskegon Mohawks in 1965. The Mohawks operated until 1984, when the team was again renamed the Muskegon Lumberjacks. The Lumberjack franchise moved to Cleveland, Ohio, in 1992, but the Muskegon Fury were quickly established to keep local ice hockey alive. The Fury played in the Colonial Hockey league until 1997, then with the United Hockey League from 1997 to 2007 (winning four championships) and currently are members of the "new" International Hockey League.

Muskegon Fury

The Muskegon Fury, an IHL ice hockey team, was established in Muskegon in 1992. Since their inception, the Fury has collected four Colonial Cup wins. The team won championships in 1999, 2002, 2004, and 2005. The Fury staff includes head coach Bruce Ramsay, general manager Tony Lisman and owner John Butler. Games are held at the L.C. Walker Arena in downtown Muskegon. 955 Fourth Street. Box Office: (231) 726-2400. www.furyhockey.com

Muskegon Thunder

The Muskegon Thunder is a member of the Continental Indoor Football League founded in Muskegon in 2007. The team plays its home games at the L.C. Walker Arena under President Don Pringle and Head Coach Shane Fairfield. 955 Fourth Street. Box Office: (231) 726-2400. www.muskegon thunder.com

RECREATION CENTERS

From sunny beaches to indoor hockey, bike trails, skiing, kayaking and fishing, Muskegon is a great place to unwind. You are only minutes away from golf courses, go-kart racing, sailing, bowling, disc golf and bowling. For further information on outdoor recreation, hiking and biking, ORV and motorcycle trails, canoe liveries, scenic drives, the Winter Sports Complex and beaches and parks, please refer to the Great Outdoor and Seafaring sections of this guidebook. Skip forward to the Michigan's Adventure section for a complete guide to Michigan's favorite theme park. Ready? Let's Go!

L.C. Walker Arena
A major sports and entertainment venue, L.C. Walker Arena at Fourth Street and West Western Avenue is a good place for the family to catch a hockey or football game or enjoy ice skating. Longtime hometown International Hockey League favorites, the Muskegon Fury play here in the fall, winter and spring. The Muskegon Thunder has introduced indoor football. The arena can accommodate up to 5,100 people in its "comfort seating" for hockey games and many other events. Public ice skating is open Saturdays 2:00 p.m. to 4:00 p.m. except when preempted by major events. Admission is $3, and skate rental is $4. Parties of 10 or more get $1 per person off admission. For event schedule information, call (231) 726-2939 or visit www.lcwalkerarena.com. The box office is open from 9:00 a.m. to 5:00 p.m. Monday through Friday.

The Muskegon Trolley Company

The whole family will love this old-fashioned tour of Muskegon County. The trolley will stop at any safe street corner along the route. At 25 cents per person, it's quite possibly the cheapest thrill in town! Trolleys run Monday through Saturday, Memorial Day through Labor Day, 9:30 a.m. to 6:30 p.m. 2624 Sixth Street. (231) 724-6420. Visit www.matsbus.com for complete route and stop information.

Muskegon YMCA

Affordable and centrally located, this lakeshore complex is ideal year-round. A gym, weight room, squash court, running track and a cardio room with ellipticals, treadmills, stepping machines and stationary bikes make it easy to keep up your personal exercise program. Members can take a run on indoor tracks or swim—laps or leisure—in the Olympic-size indoor swimming pool. Positioned below the indoor track is a full-size gymnasium where the whole family can participate in volleyball or basketball. Afterward, relax in the complete steam room, sauna and whirlpool facilities. Massage and laundry services are also available. While at least a monthly membership is required, affordable rates for families are available. Membership benefits include free access to aerobic and water exercise classes, racquetball courts and nursery services.

Kids can have fun in the game room or in the indoor Youth Zone play place. In the warm season, the little ones can head outside to a playground with lots of fun, active equipment where kids can have a ball.

A well-run health and exercise center, the Y offers clean, well-maintained facilities. Building hours are Monday through Friday 5:30 a.m. to 10:00 p.m., Saturday 6:00 a.m. to

6:00 p.m., and Sundays 12:00 noon to 5:00 p.m. Pool hours: Monday through Friday 5:30 a.m. to 9:45 p.m., Saturday 6:00 a.m. to 5:45 p.m. and Sunday 12:00 noon to 4:45 p.m. Nursery hours: Monday through Friday 8:00 a.m. to 1:00 p.m. and 4:00 to 8:00 p.m., and Saturdays 8:00 a.m. to 1:00 p.m. (231) 722-9322. www.muskegonymca.org

Lakeshore Sports Centre
Enjoy winter with this complex's indoor hockey, public skating, soccer and hockey leagues. Two NHL-size hockey rinks and an indoor soccer/flag football field are always busy. Heated rinkside seating, a children's arcade and full service concession stand add to the fun. Skates, sticks and pucks are available for rental. Drop-in prices vary. 4470 Airline Road. Call (231) 739-9423 for up to date information on fees and schedules. www.lakeshoresportscentre.com

DAY CARE

Orchard View Day Camp
If you're looking for a day camp for your children, try Orchard View Schools. They offer a summer child care camp at Cardinal Elementary School from June 9 through August 22 for children ages 6 to 12. The campers take field trips on Tuesdays and Thursdays and spend the day at the pool on Fridays. Costs run $125 for five days, $85 for three days and $35 for one day. Parents can also get a 50-percent discount for enrolling two children at the camp. These prices include breakfast, lunch and a snack for each camper. 2310 Marquette Avenue. (231) 760-1350.

LASSIE STEAL HOME

In the film *A League of Their Own*, Madonna and Geena Davis join a professional girls' baseball team formed during World War II to help quench fans' thirst for their favorite sport. Not a bad substitute for the men who had gone off to war, the real All American Girls Professional Baseball League came to Muskegon in 1946. Based at Marsh Field, the Muskegon Lassies captured a pennant in 1947, knocking off Grand Rapids and Racine, Wisconsin. Led by star pitcher and outfielder Doris Sams, who opened the 1948 season with a no-hitter, the Lassies played on until 1950 when they moved to Kalamazoo. Although the league closed in 1954, the Lassies remain an important Muskegon athletic tradition, a step ahead of the Title IX era that has brought women's sports to every school in the community.

Salvation Army Day Camp

This camp also runs from June 9 through August 22 for children ages 6 to 12. Campers take field trips, do arts and crafts projects, visit many of the state parks and museums and go to local lakes for swimming. They also do bible study every day. Costs run $75 per week, with each additional child costing $60. Breakfast, lunch and a snack are included in the price. 1221 Shonat Street. (231) 773-3824.

SKATING

Roller Skating Rinks:
Jumpin' Jupiter Skating Center: 1775 Evanston Avenue. (231) 773-5538. www.jumpinjupiter.net
Roller Fox: 12189 East Apple Avenue, Ravenna. (231) 853-2971. www.rollerfox.com

Ice Skating Rinks:
Lakeshore Sports Centre: 4470 Airline Highway. (231) 739-9423. www.lakeshoresportscentre.com
L.C. Walker Arena: Public ice skating is open Saturdays 2:00 p.m. to 4:00 p.m. when there are no events taking place. Admission $3, skate rental $4. 955 Fourth Street. (231) 726-2939. See earlier listing. www.lcwalkerarena.com

Craig's Cruisers Family Fun Center
Located a few minutes south of the Lakes Mall, this indoor and outdoor center will delight everyone in the family with go-kart racing, mini-golf, laser tag, bumper boats and an arcade. A great choice for a birthday party. 1551 East Pontaluna Road, Spring Lake. Just off US 31. (231) 798-4836. www.craigscruisers.com

FARMS, U-PICKS AND STABLES

Rainbow Ranch Horseback Riding Stables
Just a 30-minute scenic drive north on US 31, Rainbow Ranch offers over 300 acres of private woods, rivers and trails. Riders of all ages and abilities can enjoy an afternoon of guided horseback riding in this rural retreat. Horse-drawn hay rides, sleigh and carriage rides and pony rides round out the selection. Hot dog roasts add to the fun. Prices vary. 4345 S. 44th Avenue, New Era. (231) 861-4445. www.rainbowranch-inc.com.

Creswick Farms
Growers and suppliers of all-natural meats, Creswick Farms offers tour by advance arrangement. While you're there you can purchase grassfed beef and lamb, fresh-air heritage pork, pasturized chicken, free-range brown eggs, Thanksgiving turkeys, smoked meats and specialty sausages. Please call ahead. Hours vary seasonally. 6500 Rollenhagen Road, Ravenna. (616) 837-9226. www.creswickfarms.com

Country Dairy, Inc. & Farm Store
Michigan locals love Country Dairy for its BST (bovine growth hormone) free milk, cheese, butter and premium ice cream. Don't miss a chance to tour the farm and enjoy a bottomless cup of Country Dairy milk. Cold and hot sandwiches, wraps, grilled panini sandwiches and hoagies offered in the farm store and deli make a lovely lunch during your travels. Top things off with a specialty sundae or choose from 17 flavors of one of Michigan's favorite ice cream brands, made right on the farm. Farm store and visitor's center open Mon-

day through Saturday 7:00 a.m. to 10:00 p.m. 3476 South 80th Avenue, New Era. (231) 861-4636. www.countrydairy.com

Dave's Harvest
A good bet for u-pick peaches, apples and sweet cherries, Dave's also offers a wide variety of other fruits and vegetables—a handy stop on your way back from a day on the Muskegon River. Open daily May through October. 17485 Apple Avenue, Casnovia. (616) 675-5384.

Double JJ Ranch & Golf Resort
Double JJ is big enough to be broken down into three separate areas, designed specifically for kids, families and groups. A wide range of lodging, dining and camping facilities are available in all price ranges. This complex offers an RV park, family cabins, log homes, condos, hotels and suites. You can also find horses, a barn/petting farm and a swimmin' hole with a 150-foot slide. The Double JJ boasts a championship golf course, a large indoor waterpark and a restaurant and saloon. The resort hosts the Fourth of July Rothbury Festival, featuring more than 70 musical groups. 5900 Water Road, Rothbury. (800) 366-2535. www.doublejj.com

Hyatt Blueberry Farm
This farm is a great place to take the whole family. Open July through mid-September, Monday through Saturday 8:30 a.m. to dusk, Sundays by appointment only. 6082 Zeller Road, Whitehall. (231) 893-8965.

Lewis' Farm Market and Petting Zoo
Head to Lewis' for seasonally delicious u-pick fruits and

vegetables, ranging from asparagus in the spring to straw-berries in June and Michigan's famous cherries in July—and, of course, 20 varieties of apples in the fall. Lewis' also features a bakery and petting farm. Open May through October. 4180 West M-20, New Era. (231) 861-5730. www.lewis farmmarket.com

Lothschutz Farms
Lothschutz offers u-pick blueberry fields and over-the-counter sales south of Twin Lake. Open from July 20 to August 20, weekdays 9:00 a.m. to 5:30 p.m. and 8:00 a.m. to 12:00 noon weekends. 4080 Holton Road. (231) 744-0160 or (231) 740-7354.

Rennhack Orchards Market
Just off the Hart exit on US 31 north of Muskegon, stop in at Rennhack's for a selection of apples, cherries, peaches, nectarines, plums, vine-ripened tomatoes and fresh picked sweet corn. Rennhack's market also features a full line of jams, maple syrup, dried fruit, cherry juice, blueberry products and specialty items. 3731 West Polk Road, Hart. (231) 873-7523. www.rennhackorchardsmarket.com

Magicland Farms
Magicland Farms prides itself on farm-grown vegetables and fruits. Everything they sell is grown on site, including sweet corn, tomatoes and red potatoes, pumpkins, black walnuts, pecans and apples. Visit the craft room and pick up some fall decorations. 4380 South Gordon, Fremont. (231) 652-2368. www.magiclandfarms.com

Heritage Farms and Market
Don't miss this family favorite just off M-120. In autumn, bring the kids to explore the corn maze or romp in the large pumpkin patches, where they can choose their own for carving. Afterward, enjoy homemade donuts and cider poured fresh from the press right in front of your eyes. Hayrides and a delicious selection of bakery goods, market gifts, jams, pure maple syrup, Country Dairy milks and cheeses, bulk spices and popcorn and candy will ensure everyone goes home happy. 1888 South Maple Island Road, Fremont. (231) 854-3276. www.heritagefarmsandmarket.com

Christmas Tree Farms:
Windy Pines is a great "choose and cut" Christmas tree farm just fifteen minutes north of Muskegon—the place to take the kids to pick out a perfect pine at a good price. A popular family tradition, Windy Pines also features a small gift shop. Highly recommended. 4271 Putnam Road. (231) 766-3553.

   Montague Tree Farms, another good option, offers blue spruce, Scotch pine and Douglas fir, as well as holiday wreaths. 3220 Fruitvale Road, Montague. (231) 894-2020. www.montaguetreefarms.com

GOLF COURSES

Affordable, uncrowded and challenging, Muskegon's golf courses are also local scenic highlights. With a dozen first-rate choices, this region is a great place to plan a golf vacation. All the courses recommended here are popular with locals and visitors alike. Not on our list is the estimable Muskegon Country Club, where you need a member to sponsor you.

Bent Pine Golf Club
Its fairways lined with lush stands of maples and pines, this course has cart rentals and senior rates. 18 holes, 6,021 yards. 2480 Duck Lake Road, Whitehall. (231) 766-2045.

Chase Hammond Golf Club
Designed by Mark DeVries, this scenic course with its tree-lined fairways has been a local favorite since it opened in 1969. 18 holes, 6,015 yards, par 72. 2454 Putnam Road, North Muskegon. (231) 766-3035. www.chasehammond golfclub.com

Eagle Island Golf Club
Built in 1997, this executive golf course also has a practice facility. 9 holes, 2,901 yards, par 34. 800 South Mill Iron Road. (231) 733-7171.

Fruitport Golf Club
One of the area's best, this walk-or-ride course built in 1972 features elevated tees and greens. 18 holes, 5,725 yards. 6334 South Harvey. (231) 798-3355. www.fruitportgolfclub.com

Hickory Knoll Golf Course
Ponds, rolling terrain, uneven lies and dogleg fairways make this one of the most challenging courses in the Muskegon area. 36 holes, three courses. 3065 Alice Street, Whitehall. (231) 894-5535.

Moss Ridge Golf Club
Designed by W. Bruce Matthers III, this course is set apart by its luxuriant bentgrass fairways, tees and greens. It also

has complete practice facilities. 18 holes, 6,943 yards. 13545 Apple Avenue (M-46), Ravenna. (231) 853-5665. www. mossridge.com

Oak Ridge Golf Course
Built in 1937, this course has a short layout. 18 holes, 6,010 yards, par 73. 513 West Pontaluna. (231) 798-3360.

Old Channel Trail Golf Course
These lakefront links include the Muskegon area's oldest golf course, the Woods Course, built in 1926 with Scottish-style bunkers and now surrounded by many tall trees. Since then, the parklike Meadow Course and the intricate Valley Course, intertwined with a natural ravine and water hazards, have been added. 27 holes. 8325 North Old Channel Trail, Montague. (231) 894-5076. www.octgolf.com

Ravenna Creeks Golf Course
This course, designed by Doug Barthalow, has been a local favorite since 1981. 18 holes, 6,137 yards, par 72. 11566 Ravenna Heights Road, Ravenna. (231) 853-6736.

Stonegate Golf Club
One of Michigan's top championship courses, the club also has a short game practice facility and top-notch instructors. 18 holes, 6,878 yards. 4110 Sweeter Road, Twin Lake. (231) 744-7200. www.stonegategolfclub.com

University Park Golf Course
Built in 1976, this is the closest course to downtown Muskegon. Its wooded, hilly location makes for a challenging

short game. There is also a driving range as well as a practice green. 9 holes. 2100 Marquette Avenue. (231) 773-0023.

West Wind Golf Course
Built in 1999, this is one of the newer championship courses in the area. 18 holes, 5,302 yards, par 72. 2644 East Hile Road. (231) 733-8814.

Miniature Golf
Miniature golf is always a great family activity. Muskegon has four first-rate courses. They include:
Bat'n Club Mini Golf: 2544 Barclay Street. (231) 759-7723.
Craig's Cruisers Family Fun Center: 1551 East Pontaluna Road, Spring Lake. Just off US 31. (231) 798-4836. www.craigscruisers.com
Putters Creek Mini Golf: 40 Causeway, North Muskegon. (231) 744-1418.
Rocky Point Mini-Golf: Michigan's Adventure, 4750 Whitehall Road. (231) 766-3377. www.miadventure.com

BOWLING

Bowling is a hometown sport in this community, which has enjoyed a long and mutually beneficial relationship with the Brunswick Corporation. Although this company has moved bowling ball production to Mexico, Brunswick continues to maintain finance and development offices locally.
AMF Muskegon Lanes: 1150 Whitehall Road, North Muskegon. (231) 744-2451. www.amf.com
Bob Hi Lanes: 2930 South Getty. (231) 733-1928.

Hackley House (foreground) and Hume House

Pere Marquette Beach

Muskegon Channel Lighthouse

Sailing on Lake Michigan

Stewart Shell at Blue Lake Fine Arts Camp

Michigan's Adventure

White Lake Lighthouse

Pastoral byways

Muskegon Channel Lighthouse at sunset

Northway Lanes & Billiards: 1751 Evanston. (231) 767-2695. www.northwaylanesbowlingalley.com
Sherman Bowling Center & Billiards: 1531 West Sherman Boulevard. (231) 755-1258. www.shermanbowlingcenter. com

STOCK CAR AND MOTORCYCLE RACING

Thunderbird Race Park
Enjoy circle track, drag and motocross racing. 350 W Riley Thompson Road. (231) 766-3300. www.thunderbird racepark.com

Winston Motor Speedway
Stock car racing and the Lake Shore Demolition are all popular here. 7834 S 72nd Avenue, Rothbury. (231) 719-0326. www.winstonmotorspeedway.com

Muskegon Sandbox
Dirt bike fans, don't miss this one—supercross, motocross and quad racing on a dirt track. All skill levels and ages are welcome. Concessions on site. 5718 Putnam Road, North Muskegon. (231) 766-2576. www.muskegonsandbox.com

National Pro Hill Climb
Hosted by the Muskegon Motorcycle Club, this major bikers' event takes place in July at Mt. Garfield on Lake Harbor Road. www.muskegonbiketime.com

SHERMAN POPPEN:
FATHER OF THE SNOWBOARD

In 1965, Sherman Poppen, a chemical engineer living in Muskegon, invented an early model of the snowboard when he tied two skis together and placed a steering rope near the front for his daughter Wendy. Sherman's wife playfully dubbed it a "Snurfer," a mix between snow and surfer. Sherman found a manufacturer when Wendy's friends wanted to try it themselves; he began selling Snurfers for $15 a pop. Sales soared and hit 500,000 a year. Jake Burton Carpenter of Burton Boards later redeveloped Sherman's design into what we now know as the snowboard.

LAKESIDE DISTRICT AND THE CHANNEL

L akeside is a great little waterfront community nestled just two miles west of Muskegon's downtown. The arrival of the *Lake Express* ferry has made this neighborhood a point of entry for tens of thousands of new visitors each summer. But Lakeside is also well known for its marinas, which draw sailors and power boat owners from throughout the Midwest. The addition of the Lakeshore Trail also makes this neighborhood a popular jump off point for biking trips around Muskegon Lake. Art galleries and the revival of the popular Harbor Theater make this an up-and-coming area with easy access to the ever popular lakeshore. From sailboat rentals to foreign films, the Lakeshore District is a Muskegon Best Bet.

Harbor Theater

A Muskegon tradition, now operating as a nonprofit, the Harbor is the place for new releases, art films, treasured classics, film festivals, children's theater and workshops. An excellent value, the Harbor is located at 1937 Lakeshore Drive. (231) 457-4273.

SHOPPING & GALLERIES

The Lakeside District is a good place for casual browsing at small galleries like **Art Cats**, which features the work of over 30 artists, including owner Louise Hopson. 1845 Lakeshore Drive. (231) 755-7606. A Muskegon Best Bet. See our more extensive listing in the shopping section. www.artcatsgallery.com. Nearby **Lakeside Dune Glass** features blown glass gifts, demonstrations, sales, gallery of gifts, paintings and stained glass. 1812 Lakeshore Drive. (231) 755-0328. In the same building, **Lost Treasures of the Great Lakes** specializes in decoys, carved hunting pieces and cottage art. 1812 Lakeshore Drive. (231) 638-6048. Also here is **Through the Looking Glass**, an art gallery, studio and gift boutique featuring local artists. 1812 Lakeshore Drive. (231) 282-1152.

SPECIALTY MARKETS

Ghezzi's Market

Ghezzi's offers a wide selection of wines, liquors, beers and specialty foods as well as out of town papers. Ghezzi's also has a small deli selection with cheeses and meats. Wine and beer selections feature local breweries and wineries from across the state. Ghezzi's also offers a nice selection of Michigan-made dips, marinades, dressings and other specialties. 2017 Lakeshore Drive. (231) 755-3479.

Lakeside Emporium
Nestled in the center of the Lakeside neighborhood, this shop features licorice, popcorn, Jelly Bellys, Slo Pokes, Chick-o-Sticks, and Teaberry gum. The homemade fudge has a loyal following. Kids and adults will have fun shuffling through the assortment of treats. 1929 Lakeshore Drive. (231) 755-9933. www.lakeside-emporium.com

A VAUDEVILLE LEGEND ON THE LAKESHORE

Muskegon played host to a colony of vaudeville actors near the turn of the century, most notably Buster Keaton. Just like the thousands of visitors who come back every year, Keaton was drawn to the laid back vibe of the Muskegon shoreline and its inhabitants. In his biography he quietly observes that, "The best summers of my life were spent in the cottage Pop had built on Lake Muskegon in 1908." Keaton came back to the area every summer after that, helping to develop a Muskegonite community of comedic performers which survived until 1938 when the film industry made vaudeville nearly obsolete. But the Muskegon area has not forgotten Buster Keaton; a monument in his name stands on the lakeshore in the spot he used to love. Each fall, an annual convention of The Damfinos—The International Buster Keaton Society—draws vaudeville lovers from all over the world to view screenings of Keaton's films at the Frauenthal Theater downtown.

SEAFARING

West Michigan's largest deepwater port is a lively transportation hub where freighters, high-speed ferries, cruise ships, cigar boats, Jet Skis and sailboats peacefully coexist. Thanks to numerous inland lakes the region also offers many quiet nautical byways. Freighters carrying lots of coal, aggregate, cement and iron ore are ever present during the shipping season. Arrival and departure times are posted in the *Chronicle* and at www.visitmuskegon.com, which offers a web cam look at nautical traffic.

PORT CITY PRINCESS

This retired Mackinac ferry is a great way to see the lakeshore in style. Enjoy a dinner cruise, or book your party for a special themed cruise. The *Princess* sails May through October and docks at 560 Mart Street. (231) 728-8387. www. portcityprincesscruises.com

SAILING AND RACING

Muskegon Lake is one of the best sailing lakes in the state. Prevailing winds virtually guarantee dependable sailing conditions on Muskegon Lake and Lake Michigan.

Even if you don't want to man the helm, you can easily watch weekend sailboat races and regattas. Check www. sailmuskegon.com for links to race clubs and schedules. Highlights include the Clipper Cup, which sends sailors on a 68.4-mile trip to Port Washington, Wisconsin. (616) 669-5333. www.clippercup.com

Torresen Marine
This sailboat marina doesn't just give you a place to store and dock your boat; you can take ASA certified sailing lessons and set out on the Great Lakes. Torresen also offers a sailing ships store and a full list of services. 3003 Lake Shore Drive. (231) 759-8596. www.torresen.com. Torresen's webcam gives you a quick view of Muskegon Lake conditions. www.torresen.com/aboutUs.php?p=webCam &title=Muskegon+Lake+Web+Cam+Camera+View+of+ Muskegon+Michigan

West Michigan Yacht Charters, LLC
Bare boat and sailing trips will take your breath away along the shores of Lake Michigan or watching the coastline from

the confines of Muskegon Lake. 13351 Lakeshore Drive. (616) 402-4665.

Dewey Sailboat Charters
Choose your poison: morning, afternoon or sunset, and the destination is up to you. Dewey's vessel sails out of Moxie Marina. 213 South Lake Street, Whitehall. (231) 670-3685.

Sorry Charlie Charters
In addition to charter fishing and scenic cruises, Sorry Charlie offers scuba diving trips. Whitehall. (231) 894-9162.

South Shore Marina and Dockside Grill
After renting a boat for a day on White Lake, head back to the harbor for drinks and dinner at the Dockside Grill. 6806 South Shore Drive, Whitehall. (231) 893-3935.

Muskegon Yacht Club Sailing School
The yacht club also offers classes at all skill levels. 3198 Edgewater. (231) 755-1414. www.muskegonyachtclub.org

FISHING

"There are only two kinds of fishing—good fishing and great fishing. Great fishing is when you actually catch something."
—Jeff McNelly

In Muskegon, great fishing is a pleasure year-round. With a little planning you really will catch something. In fact, experienced anglers report this region compares favorably to better known fishing hot spots.

From a five-year-old and her grandmother fishing off the Lake Michigan channel breakwater to driftboating virtuosos fly-casting their way down the Muskegon River, this region is an angler's paradise. Flying in from as far away as Europe and China on an annual basis, people who are serious about fishing know the Muskegon area is a pleasure. In fact much of the best fishing takes place outside the peak summer season when lodging rates are down, campgrounds are wide open and, of course, the best fishing locales such as the Muskegon River are blissfully uncrowded. Thankfully you don't need to know much about fishing to have a great time and make a great catch.

If you're new to the area and want to be relatively sure of initial success, why not check out one of the several dozen charter operations that offer everything from salmon fishing party boat trips to guided river excursions complete with a riverside barbecue lunch. The **Muskegon Charter Boat Association** at P.O. Box 211, Muskegon 49443 (231) 769-7032. www.muskegoncharterboats.com. You will also need a fishing license which can be obtained at local fishing shops and retailers or online at www.mdnr-elicense.com/welcome. asp. For a quick look at lake fishing seasons between April and October for chinook and coho salmon, steelhead and rainbow trout, brown trout and lake trout visit www.muskegoncharterboats.com/fishing.htm. Additional charter boat and fishing guide listings are available at www.visitmuskegon.org/charters.cfm. You may also want to check the weekly state Division of Natural Resources Fishing report for a handy update on local conditions. www.michigan.gov/dnr/0,1607,7-153-10364---,00.html. You'll also find statewide fishing information at www.great-lakes.org/fish_mi.html.

A great place to get started, if you prefer to fish from the shore, is **Shoreline Service Bait and Tackle** at 2080 Lakeshore Drive. (231) 759-7254. It's just minutes from prime Muskegon and Lake Michigan fishing spots. Muskegon Lake, which has benefited from a remarkable cleanup effort in recent years, is blessed with a myriad of species including salmon, trout, whitefish, walleye, bass, bluegills and pike. A good starting point is **Snug Harbor Bait Shop** near a prime Muskegon Lake launch point on the east side of Muskegon State Park. 3492 Memorial Drive, North Muskegon. (231) 744-3440. The lakefront has plenty of first-class fishing spots. A popular stretch parallels the shoreline heading south from the Snug Harbor launch ramp to the Lake Michigan Channel. It's set against a scenic dune backdrop. The Nature Center off Lake Street, just west of the causeway, is another good bet. You can also fish from the bridges along the bike path that links Muskegon to North Muskegon via the causeway.

The Muskegon and White Lake Channels, the southern Lake Michigan breakwater at Pere Marquette Beach or north breakwater at Muskegon State Park are ideal. An excellent choice with good wheelchair access is the 131-foot fishing bridge across the White River that links Whitehall and Montague. Bob Kingsley, who writes an admirable weekly fishing column for the *Muskegon Chronicle*, considers this an ideal location to cast for chinook salmon or fresh-run steelhead. He points out that every fish headed up the White River heads passes this spot. "You don't have to arrive early," says Kingsley, "The fish bite most any time except when the sun is directly overhead."

Another way to approach this tributary is the **White River Campground** and **Happy Mohawk Canoe Livery** at

735 Fruitvale Road. The campground is at (231) 894-4708, and you can reach the canoe livery at (231) 894-4209. www.happymohawk.com

If you don't have your own boat, there are several handy local options. **South Shore Marina** rents boats for $100 to $275 per day. 6806 South Shore Drive, Whitehall. (231) 893-3935. Another good bet is to rent a drift boat on the Muskegon River at **Wisner Canoe Rental**, open daily from April through October and weekdays from November through March. Jeff Alexander, author of *The Muskegon*, considers the stretch from Croton Dam down to Thornapple Landing in Newaygo to be the region's definitive year-round fishing spot. Here you'll find easy access to a September salmon run, steelhead running from October or November through May, as well as rainbow trout and night fishing for walleye. Tug-of-war battles make sport fishing here a great adventure. For fishing supplies, stop off at **Parsley's Sport Shop**, 70 State Road, Newaygo. (231) 652-6986.

You may be surprised to learn that salmon fishing is often better in the river than it is on Lake Michigan. Alexander, who is writing a book on invasive species in the Great Lakes, explains that zebra mussels have done a great job of cleaning up Lake Michigan and improving water clarity. Unfortunately they have also gobbled up a lot of the species that salmon feed on. The result has been a kind of Weight Watchers diet for the popular species, which no longer top out in the 30-pound-plus range. If you do decide to fish for salmon on Lake Michigan consider the advantages of a party boat guided by a knowledgeable skipper.

Among the many other popular fishing spots around the region are Fisherman's Landing, the beach off Hoffmaster

State Park, the Nature Center off Lake Street in North Muskegon (just west of the causeway) and for families with small children, Duck Lake. Other relatively quiet waters worth a try are Blue Lake, Fremont Lake, Wolf Lake and Twin Lake. Here are some of the charter operators and guides that can help you on your way. Remember, if you're new to the area these pros will put you safely on your way.

Addiction Charters: Bluffton Bay Marina, 3040 Lakeshore Drive (231) 937-9610. www.addictioncharters.com

Art's Steelhead Charters: Point Marine, North Muskegon. (231) 329-2117

Fishtale Charters: 1304 Becker. (231) 744-8156.

Great Lakes Guide Service: 1963 Bonneville. (231) 638-5752. www.glguideservice.com

Margie J Sport Fishing Charters: 4856 Laurel Street. (231) 799-2229. www.fishmuskegon.com

Navi-Gater Charters: 3278 West McMillan Road. (231) 206-5404.

North Muskegon Charters: 5048 West McMillan Road. (231) 766-9141. www.nmcharters.com

Pigs Eye Guide Service: 1317 Sherwood Drive. (231) 578-9523.

Run-N-Gun Charters: 2900 Slocum Road, Ravenna. (231) 740-7697. www.rngcharters.com

MARINAS AND CHARTERS

Bluffton Bay Marina
Several fishing charters and pleasure cruises, including Addiction Charters (231-937-9610) operate out of this marina. 3040 Lakeshore Drive. (231) 796-7032.

Great Lakes Marina and Boat Sales
This full-service marina offers slips, storage, in-out service, fuel dock and boat sales. (231) 759-8230.

Torresen Marine
One of the largest and most respected marinas in west Michigan, this is sailor haven. A sailing school and rentals complement the ships store, which serves local mariners and tourists alike. From Sunfish daytrippers to racing crews headed to Mackinac Island, this is the place to get started. Torreson's enthusiastic national clientele shops at www.torresen.com. (231) 759-8596.

RAYMOR FISH PRODUCTS

For a sample of the best in regional seafood, this local favorite is a good place to find walleye, perch, whitefish, salmon and trout. Raymor is open year-round, even when the fish aren't biting. 1449 W. Sherman Boulevard. (231) 759-3208.

LAUNCH RAMPS

Trailering boats to the Muskegon area is a longstanding tradition. From small craft to major vessels, the city offers many fine choices. Other enthusiasts prefer to store their boats here and commute on weekends and vacations. Make sure to visit www.visitmuskegon.org/marinas.htm for links to each site and more information.

Deremo Access Site
This paved launch ramp is used for boating, water-skiing and fishing. Fruitvale Road, Montague, on the north side of Big Blue Lake. (231) 744-3580.

Duck Lake State Park
This day-use state park offers fishing, hiking, swimming, picnicking and hunting. 3560 Memorial Drive, North Muskegon. (231) 744-3480.

Muskegon Lake Access
There are no less than seven launch ramps on the lake, including Grand Trunk, Hartshorn Marina, Cottage Grove, Fisherman's Landing, Jaycee's Launch Ramp, Lakeshore Launch Ramp, Muskegon State Park. www.visitmuskegon.org/marinas.htm

White Lake Launch Ramp
Boaters here will find a fish cleaning station and rest rooms. There is a daily user's fee. Launch Ramp Road, Montague. (231) 893-1155.

MUSIC AND ENTERTAINMENT

Just under Muskegon's quiet surface lies an exciting and lively life in music—even if you have to dig around a bit to locate it. Muskegon may not appear to be a music "mecca" on its surface, but a wide variety of live music and entertainment is available throughout the area. No matter what your preference—jazz, rock, dancing, symphonies or just pop cover standards—you can find it here. The Muskegon area has a rich and lasting music culture and boasts excellence in its high school music programs and professional orchestras and bands. In addition, Muskegon is no stranger to the theater arts and plays host to a kaleidoscope of stage plays and musicals.

750 Grill Room
Don't miss Muskegon's host of open mic night, where local and regional talent convene to show their stuff. The open

mic crowd tends to be young; this is definitely a party atmosphere. Check back on the weekends for information about live music and specials. Try weeknights for a more laid-back atmosphere. And 750 isn't just a bar; it won Best Booth at the 2007 Taste of Muskegon festival for its great menu options. Smoke-free. 2190 Whitehall Road, North Muskegon. (231) 744-7507.

Alley Door Club
Located on the third floor of the Frauenthal Building downtown, the Alley Door Club is a hip gathering spot for blues, rock, jazz and soul lovers. January through May on the second and fourth Fridays of the month. Happy hour starts at 6:00 p.m. with a cash bar and Muskegon's famous Ed's Barbeque on hand. The cover is $5 at the door. Enter through the alley between the Chronicle and Frauenthal buildings (off Third Street between Western and Clay) and take the elevator to the third floor. (231) 722-9750.

MUSKEGON'S GODFATHER OF PUNK

Who says big things don't come from little towns? Muskegon birthed the "Godfather of Punk," Iggy Pop. That's right. The lead singer of the Stooges was spawned in good old Muskegon. Though he lived out his school years in the Ann Arbor area and eventually moved to Chicago, Muskegonites still like to think of him as their own.

Bear Lake Tavern

On the channel between Bear Lake and Muskegon Lake, the BLT offers a great vantage point year-round. In the warm months you'll have a view of the marine traffic. In business for over 60 years, the BLT is also a popular breakfast spot, serving a variety of seafood dishes and burgers. 360 Ruddiman Avenue, North Muskegon. (231) 744-1161.

Cuti's Sports Bar & Grill

This local dive features billiards, darts, live music and TVs. 677 West Laketon Avenue. (231) 722-0033.

Glenside Pub

Stop in for a drink and pizza, Always a busy spot on the weekends. 1508 West Sherman Boulevard. (231) 759-8525.

Hobo's

Winner of Best Restaurant in Muskegon's Taste of Muskegon 2007, Hobo's is more than just a great place to go out. It has an extensive beer selection on tap and fabulous martinis. A display kitchen serves up a wide ranging menu including gourmet burgers, deluxe salads and hearty stews. There's an open-air patio in the summer. Hobo's features live music every Thursday night with Buddy Pops. 1411 Whitehall Road, North Muskegon. (231) 719-0247.

Lakeshore Tavern

This friendly favorite features affordable drinks and live music, right on the waterfront in Lakeside. 1963 Lakeshore Drive. (231) 759-7604.

The Landmark Bar & Grill
Great beer specials, an all-American menu, live bands and karaoke make this bar a local favorite, always busy on the weekends. 1308 West Sherman Boulevard. (231) 755-6818.

Local Pub
New owners have upgraded this century-old bar, adding live music on weekends and new decor that highlights the historic charm of this port city. A good bet before or after a concert at the Howmet Theater. There's a light menu offering burgers, barbecue sandwiches and perch. 111 W. Colby Street, Whitehall. (231) 894-8269.

Michillinda
Michillinda Lodge is the perfect garden setting for a drink at sunset. This establishment, one of the region's most popular resorts, has a great patio and easy access to the beach below. It's ideal for a summer gathering. 207 Scenic Drive, Whitehall. (231) 893-1895.

Marine Tap Room
Owned by Muskegon's mayor, Steve Warmington, a dedicated biker, this place rocks during the Bike Time weekend. Live bands play on the weekends. 1983 Lakeshore Drive. (231) 755-5581.

Pints & Quarts Pub and Grill
Locals love Pints & Quarts for its delicious lunch and dinner menu. It's also a nighttime favorite. From business lunches to hot dates, Pints & Quarts is a smart choice. A high

class sports bar, this classy venue features live music on the weekends, a patio and a happy hour Monday through Friday from 3:00 p.m. to 7:00 p.m. 950 West Norton, Roosevelt Park. (231) 830-9889. www.pintsandquarts.com

Red Rooster
A popular stop for a nightcap on Scenic Drive between Muskegon State Park and Duck Lake State Park, the Red Rooster features country and classic rock on Friday and Saturday nights in the summer and Saturdays in the winter months. The Oat Bran Boys are a local favorite. There's a full lunch and dinner menu. 2998 Scenic Drive. (231) 744-4006.

Tipsy Toad
This recent addition to Muskegon's downtown boasts the city's only upstairs patio dining with a view of Muskegon Lake. It features daily specials and sporting events on a big screen TV. Convenient to all downtown events, it's also a good lunch choice. 609 West Western Avenue. (231) 725-7181.

Coopersville Farm Museum Jam and Open Mic Night
This one's for the whole family. Acoustic and bluegrass music fans will love it. A plethora of instruments show up for this fun event: harmonicas, basses, guitars, banjos, fiddles and mandolins, accordions and dulcimers. Year-round, on the first and third Tuesday of every month. 6:00 p.m. to 9:00 p.m. $3 admission. 75 Main Street, Historic Downtown Coopersville. (616) 997-8734.

Main Street Mardi Gras Pub Crawl

On Fat Tuesday each year, a loud and fun-loving crowd gathers to hop from one downtown pub to the next, sporting Mardi Gras beads and celebrating all night long. Begins at 5:00 p.m. at the Holiday Inn and ends who knows when at the Tipsy Toad. Visit www.downtownmuskegon.org in January for info.

Parties in the Park

Meet 3,000 to 4,000 of your closest friends at this outdoor family favorite featuring music, drinks and takeaway fare. From June through August, concertgoers convene at Hackley Park in downtown Muskegon to enjoy local and regional band performances and first-class people watching. All concerts benefit local charities. Friday evenings, 5:00 p.m. to 9:00 p.m. Check www.partiesinthepark.com for the current schedule, or call (231) 725-6333.

Grand Rapids and Grand Haven

Just a short drive away from Muskegon, nestled along the lakeshore, sits Grand Haven, a small town with a big variety of delicious food and great live music. Check out the Kirby Grill (2 Washington, 616-846-3299) to watch dueling pianos and popular local bands, then head upstairs to K2 for incredible pizza and a game of pool. The Rose Bud Bar & Grille (100 Washington, 616-846-7788) is a local favorite for dancing, and Portobello (41 Washington, 616-846-1221) is a great stop for low-key blues and jazz.

Just a 40-minute drive east on I-96 will bring you to beautiful downtown Grand Rapids, which boasts the multi-venue B.O.B.—the name stands for "Big Old Building"—with four floors of dancing, live music and comedy. Highlights include Crush and Eve, two of West Michigan's premiere upscale nightclubs; Dr. Grins, featuring comedians from all over the world; the B.O.B. brewery which shares its award-winning microbrews; and for the easygoing crowd, a traditional sports bar setting complete with billiards at Bobarino's (20 Monroe Avenue NW, 616-356-2000, www. thebob.com). This mecca of music and excitement stands in the shadow of the giant Van Andel Arena, West Michigan's largest site for hosting everything from local sporting events to national music acts. Both north and south, a plethora of bars featuring a wide variety of live music options sit within walking distance of one another.

ARTS

West Shore Symphony Orchestra
Housed in the beautiful Frauenthal Center for Performing Arts, the West Shore Symphony Orchestra is in its 67th season and is widely recognized as one of the best regional orchestras in the Midwest. The symphony is currently under the baton of celebrated maestro Scott Speck. Classical and pops concerts feature world-class soloists. Visit www.wsso. org or call (231) 726-3231 for season schedules and event information. Tickets are available at (800) 585-3737, at Star Tickets Plus locations or at the Frauenthal Theater box office. A Muskegon Best Bet.

Muskegon Community Concerts
Based in the Frauenthal Center for Performing Arts, the Muskegon Community Concerts series brings exceptional music and theater to the Muskegon area. Programs include

groups like the Presidio Brass and the Black Mountain Chorus of Wales. Tickets are available at the Frauenthal Theater Box Office or at StarTicketsPlus locations. (231) 722-6520. www.muskegonconcerts.org

West Michigan Concert WINDS
A leading Michigan community band, the West Michigan Concert WINDS is in its 28th year as a volunteer organization. The band plays all over West Michigan, frequently visiting Muskegon's Frauenthal Center for the Performing Arts. Call (616) 847-8800 or visit www.wmcw.org for updated schedule information. Tickets available at the box office for each concert event.

THEATER ARTS

Muskegon Civic Theatre
The Muskegon Civic Theatre group includes the former Civic Opera Association, Port City Playhouse and Muskegon Youth Theatre. Collectively they offer a variety of cultural theater and events. Performances are held in the Beardsley Theater or the Frauenthal Theater. Prices range from $15 to $19. Visit www.muskegoncivictheatre.org for season information, or call (231) 722-3852. Tickets are available at (800) 585-3737 or at StarTicketsPlus locations.

Howmet Playhouse
A perfect summer theater venue that has expanded into a year-round program under the leadership of actor/director Tom Harryman, this 400-seat venue showcases national and local talent and offers operas, musicals, children's theater

and more. Come early for dinner at Sam's, a good Mediterranean restaurant on Colby. 304 S. Mears, Whitehall. (231)
894-2540. www.howmetplayhouse.org

MOVIE THEATERS

Cinema Carousel Theatre
Kids will love the full-size working carousel located inside
the lobby of this megaplex movie theater. A family entertainment center is also available for pre- and post-movie fun.
4289 Grand Haven Road, Norton Shores. (231) 798-2608.
www.celebrationcinema.com

Harbor Theater
A good bet for first run, revival and art films, the Harbor
reopened as a nonprofit theater in the spring of 2008. The
convenient location makes it a handy stop after a day at
the beach. 1937 Lakeshore. (231) 457-4273 or (231) 457-4274.
www.theharbortheater.com

Getty 4 Drive-in Theatre
One of only a handful of drive-ins left in Michigan, the Getty 4, in business since 1949, offers a good look at a bygone
era when teens necked in cars, parents toting kids ignored
them and everyone ate too much popcorn. With summer
sunsets around 9:30, a trip to the Getty is the perfect alibi for
a late night out. It's also a lot of fun. The refurbished screen
makes the Getty a wise choice for those who have burned
out on Netflix and prefer to see their favorite movie stars on
the large screen. 920 Summit Avenue. (231) 798-2608. Open
April to September. www.celebrationcinema.com

113

MUSKEGON'S BIG EVENTS

The Muskegon area is bursting with celebrations, music and parties. You will be surprised by the amazing variety of events it has to offer, from motorcycle rallies to Christian music festivals, it's really all right here in Muskegon. Plan your trip around one of these great community events.

For a detailed listing of festivals and events on the Muskegon coast, consult www.muskegon.org.

FEBRUARY

Muskegon Film Festival
For three days and nights in February, independent films are presented and judged in the theaters of Muskegon's beautiful and historic Frauenthal Center for the Perform-

ing Arts. Activities include a beverage tent with live music, "snowball volleyball," and a cook-off. Tickets are available from StarTicketsPlus locations and at the Frauenthal Theater box office and range from $6 to $50. www.muskegon-filmfestival.com

MAY

Fiesta Sabor Latino
Samba and sizzle to celebrate West Michigan's Latino Heritage. Music, food, dance, vendors and a car show comprise Fiesta Sabor Latino in Downtown Muskegon's Hackley Park. Mid-May. (231) 728-3201. www.muskegonfiesta.com

Rock the Coast
Enjoy a thrill ride and rock out to Christian music during Rock the Coast at Michigan's Adventure theme park. The event takes place in mid-May. Check out www.rockthe-coast.net for updated concert info.

Lost Boat Ceremony / Blessing of the Boats
This Memorial Day weekend event takes place at the Great Lakes Naval Memorial and Museum to honor the submarines and submariners lost during World War II. A priest also blesses the U.S.S. *Silversides*, LST 393 and the *Milwaukee Clipper* as part of a weekend that includes a champagne brunch and live music. 1346 Bluff Street. (231) 755-1230. www.glnmm.org

JUNE

Muskegon Heights Festival in the Park

The community of Muskegon Heights gathers each June to celebrate together, with a senior picnic and a health fair kicking off the events. Sporting events, a parade, arts and crafts, tons of food and a gospel service make this a great little fest. (231) 578-2099.

Muskegon Main Street Car & Motorcycle Show

On an often sizzling Saturday in June, Western Avenue rumbles up and down with muscle-car exhausts and motorcycles revving at the Main Street Car & Motorcycle Show. The Muskegon show presents awards to the top autos and bikes, placing winners in 24 A-to-Z categories, including antique motors from pre-1940. www.mainstreetcarshow.com

Miss Michigan Pageant

Each June, Muskegon hosts the popular Miss Michigan Pageant at the Frauenthal Theater. Several winners have gone on to become Miss America. Among them is the 2008 winner, Kristen Haglund. www.missmichigan.org

Derbyshire Renaissance Faire

At the Muskegon County Fairgrounds on Heights-Revanna Road just west of Muskegon, the Derbyshire Renaissance Fair takes place each June. The fair events span four days, just enough time for visitors to fully enjoy all of the events taking place. Take a step back in time with Lord Drake's Mystic Illusions, with its blend of comedy and outrageousness. www.derbyshirerenfaire.com

Seaway Run

The Seaway Run takes place in Muskegon, along the shores of Lake Michigan, and is one of Michigan's most popular runs. The scenic morning race begins at the Muskegon Family YMCA, located at 900 W. Western Avenue and includes a 5K that is mostly a flat loop, a 15K run that takes participants along a slightly hilly terrain, and a newly added Walk for Fun following the Lakeshore Trail. www.mlive.com/seawayrun

Taste of Muskegon

Residents of the area are well acquainted with the exceptional selection of food in the Muskegon area; next to natural attractions, it could well be Muskegon's best kept secret. Over 11,000 hungry visitors gather around the table during the third week in June for Muskegon's annual Taste of Muskegon food festival. Acoustic and street performers keep things lively during the day, while full bands perform at night in the beverage tent. The event takes place downtown on Western Avenue between Third and Fourth Streets. www.tasteofmuskegon.com

Muskegon Summer Celebration

Muskegon's Summer Celebration takes place during the last week of June and spills into the first week of July. The grounds at Heritage Landing in downtown Muskegon host the majority of events along Muskegon's incredible lakeshore. Other events take place at historic Hackley Park and along the streets of downtown Muskegon.

Summer Celebration is a ten-day music festival. Local crowds are joined by visitors from all over the Midwest who flock to Muskegon to enjoy the party. Night after

117

night, acts like Peter Frampton, Aretha Franklin, Steve Miller, Smokey Robinson, Bonnie Raitt, The Doobie Brothers, Collective Soul and Blues Traveler entertain 625,000 people each year! The festival continues to grow and draws an increasingly impressive roster of national acts. Highlighting the area's rich musical and cultural tradition, the festival rounds itself out with local and regional bands opening for main acts and playing the secondary stages. Eleven-day passes can be purchased in advance starting in May. Bargain pricing starting at just $95 is available for adults and children. Day passes to individual concerts vary by act and seating area. www.summercelebration.com

Meijer Art in the Park: For three days 180,000 festival goers visit the Meijer Art in the Park event in Hackley Park. Running for nearly 50 years the juried show draws over 160 varied and talented artisans. As part of downtown Muskegon, Hackley Park adds a historic touch to this show.

Comerica Village Craft Market: While walking the streets of downtown Muskegon during the Comerica Village Craft Market, you can expect to find a unique handcrafted item to your liking. After 48 years running, the craft market is now made up of 180 exhibitors and continues to grow. Located on Clay Avenue from Fourth to Sixth, Sixth to Western, Western to Fourth and Fourth to Clay on the second Saturday of events, the Comerica Village Craft Market is sure to meet the whimsy of any visitor seeking handcrafted goods and gifts.

Michigan Marketplace: The ADAC Automotive Michigan Marketplace offers guests a wide variety of tastes. The homemade foods range from specialty spices to fudge, which visitors can enjoy on-site or take home.

Plumb's Annual Picnic: Bring the kids for a picnic lunch, ice cream, free games and prizes hosted by Plumb's. The largest in the state, this family picnic event occurs on the first Sunday of the festival. Admission is free, and children under 10 can play free games for prizes.

Huntington Bank Bistro: Taste a sampling of Michigan wine or relax with a gourmet brew under an umbrella at the Huntington Bank Bistro, located on the streets of downtown for the duration of the festival.

Big Rigs . . . Big Party West Michigan Truck Show: Diesel prices may be up, but that isn't stopping truckers from revving up for June's Summerfest. A bevy of semis is the heart and soul of this giant tricked-out truck show. Held in the Morris Avenue parking lot, this event features over 100 trucks and 50 vendors. The rolling thunder spectacular winds up with a morning Big Rig Parade through downtown. (231) 726-2871. www.westmichigantruckshow.com

JULY

Rothbury

In 2008, Rothbury kicked off its first year on Fourth of July weekend. With a lineup that in the past has included the Dave Matthews Band, Phil Lesh and Friends, John Mayer, Snoop Dog, Betty LaVette and dozens of other groups, the Rothbury Festival is a West Michigan sustainable camping event celebrating music, arts and action. Located just 20 minutes from downtown Muskegon at the Double JJ Ranch, Rothbury includes an environmental think tank, a circus, a theatre, yoga sessions and an environmental action program. Be forewarned; guests are strictly limited to bringing in no more than 72 cans of beer per person. With lodging ranging from the campground to Double JJ bunkhouse facilities, this summer spectacular offers tickets starting at $244 for the long Fourth of July weekend. Of course you can also enjoy Double JJ's resort attractions such as horseback riding, golf, an indoor waterpark, boating, cycling, crafts, a petting farm and target shooting. Stay at the campground, in a hotel room, condo or vacation suite. For more details on Double JJ see the Recreation section of this guide or call (800) 368-2535 or visit www.doublejj.com 5900 Water Road, Rothbury, MI 49452. (231) 368-2535. To learn more about the Rothbury Festival visit www.rothburyfestival.com

THE COOL ONE: BEER TENTS!

Muskegon may not rival Oktoberfest, but she sure lives it up under that tent year-round—rain, snow, sleet or shine. That's why she's been dubbed the "Beer Tent Capital of the World." Many tents go well beyond traditional American draft to offer specialty bottled beer. You just can't stop the partygoers here, yet the atmosphere is always lighthearted, and everyone is out to have a good time. The beverage tents appearing for Snowfest, Summer Celebration and a plethora of other events often feature live music and draft beer, as well as nonalcoholic beverages and food—usually grilled dogs and burgers. The full-hearted spirit of tent-lovers is demonstrated by the community-based Party in the Park events that occur on Friday afternoons in the height of summer. Now that's fun!

Muskegon County Fair

Located on Heights Ravenna Road in Fruitport at the Muskegon County Fairgrounds, this County Fair has something for everyone, with all of the usual events like horses, poultry, goats, swine, and dairy cattle competitions, plus "toss the pig," an egg run, tractor and truck pulls, motocross, autocross, a tractor show, a 4-H point show, pie-eating contests and a water balloon toss, among many others. This rare event should not be missed. www.muskegonfairgrounds.com

Muskegon Bike Time

During a weekend in mid-July, Muskegon offers Bike Time for tens of thousands of motorcycle enthusiasts to enjoy biker festivities. Complete with music, a motorcycle-only main street, beer tents, food, equipment vendors and national motorcycle dealers, the event began in 2007. Muskegon offers an official Bike Time campsite. The weekend includes Get Married at Muskegon Bike Time and the National Pro Hill Climb hosted by the Muskegon Motorcycle Club. www.muskegon biketime.com

Cruz'in White Lake

Watch hundreds of pre-1975 classic cars cruise a route between downtown Whitehall at City Hall and downtown Montague. The cruise winds up with a community gathering with live music. Late July. (231) 893-1155. Visit www. whitelake.org for more information.

AUGUST

Unity Christian Music Festival
Each year in August, 45 Christian bands praise the Lord through music on three different stages at Muskegon's Heritage Landing. The family-friendly festival is the largest of its kind in the state. Activities, a prayer tent and other spiritual events round out the festival attractions. Check out www.unitymusicfestival.com for current event information and links to other Christian concerts taking place in the Muskegon area throughout the year. Tickets are available online or at StarTicketsPlus locations.

Annual Moose Fest
The Annual Moose Fest takes place on the lakeshore, where thousands of music fans can enjoy country music performances. Located at Muskegon's beautiful Heritage Landing each August, admission is free and tickets are available to be picked up at local businesses. To keep up to date on this year's performers, visit www.107mus.com as the date gets closer.

SEPTEMBER

Muskegon Shoreline Spectacular
Celebrate summer one last time. On Labor Day weekend at Pere Marquette Beach, families gather to have fun and enjoy the last days of summer. Activities include an arts and crafts fair, a parade, elephant rides, carnival games, free kids' art workshops, a Frisbee dog show, and a bever-

age tent with live music every night. (231) 780-1464. www.
shorelinespectacular.org

Michigan Irish Music Festival

Located at the WaterMark Center in Heritage Landing, the
Michigan Irish Music Festival presented by Mercy General Health Partners is a mid-September weekend event
celebrating all things Irish. The public can join in on some
Irish dance classes or watch one of the Heinzman & Quinn
School of Irish Dance Performances. Festivities include Irish
music, beer, merchandise and food from the Irish market
and food court. www.michiganirish.org

DECEMBER

Heritage Holiday Home Tour

Showcasing a beautiful array of Muskegon's historic and
unique homes, the Nelson Neighborhood Association draws
hundreds to its annual Holiday Home Tour. A fresh theme
ensures a new set of homes will be chosen each year, with the
exception of historic mainstays like the Scolnik Depression
House and the Frauenthal Jefferson home. The tour begins
at the Union Depot, 610 W. Western Avenue. This one-day
tour usually takes place during the first week in December.
Tickets are $12, except for children 12 and under, who can
join the tour for free. Tickets can be purchased the day of
the tour at the Union Depot or in advance at The Frauenthal
Center Box Office, Pitkin's Drug or Keefe's Pharmacy. www.
downtownmuskegon.org/heritagehometour.shtml

Mona Shores High School Singing Christmas Tree
Located in the Frauenthal Theater in early December, the Singing Christmas Tree is the largest in the nation, and it's always a sellout show. Two hundred Mona Shores high-schoolers join the festivities to sing Christmas favorites and multicultural selections. The singing tree is accompanied by Mona Shores' accomplished Chamber Orchestra. Tickets are available for purchase in advance via Frauenthal Center's Box Office, located in the lobby of the Frauenthal Theater, or by calling (800) 585-3737. A Muskegon Best Bet.

Holiday Festival of Trees
Located at the Muskegon Museum of Art, the Holiday Festival of Trees will be sure to get you into the holiday mood. The festival includes a vast display of trees and wreaths, a gingerbread village, a Reindeer Stomp holiday party and a Teddy Bear Breakfast.

SHOPPING GUIDE

Muskegon has more to offer than nature and music. Visitors will enjoy a variety of shopping opportunities, from incredible local food markets to small clothing boutiques and fine furniture stores. Don't hesitate to peruse the area's many offerings during your stay, whether you are wandering the streets of downtown or heading out to mall country. See also the Lakeside and New Downtown sections for a list of shops in those areas.

FARMERS AND FLEA MARKETS

Muskegon Farmers and Flea Market
For a selection of the best West Michigan fruits, vegetables, flowers and plants, visit the Muskegon Farmers Market located at Yuba and Seaway Drive, Tuesday, Thursday and

Saturday mornings until 1:00 p.m., May through December. One of the largest markets in the state, this is the place where you're likely to come for a few minutes and wind up staying for an hour. A community crossroads, this farmers market is not to be missed. As the months go by, spring flowers give way to summer strawberries, replaced in turn by fresh pumpkin pie, Christmas wreaths and trees. Stop back on Wednesday between 5:00 a.m. and 3:00 p.m. to enjoy the array of antiques and collectibles at the Muskegon Flea Market. Yuba and Seaway Drive. (231) 724-6704. Truly a Muskegon Best Bet.

Muskegon Heights Farmers Market
Memorial Day weekend through August. 2724 Peck, Muskegon Heights. Wednesday, Friday and Saturday, 7:00 a.m. to 7:00 p.m. The flea market is open Tuesday and Saturday, same location and hours. (231) 724-3100.

Sweetwater Local Foods Market
A new market to the Muskegon area, the Sweetwater Local Foods Market is dedicated to selling locally grown animal products, fruits and vegetables that are raised in a humane and ecologically sustainable manner. It is also the only market open during Michigan's erratic winter months. The market carefully selects vendors who bypass synthetics fertilizers or soil treatments, chemical pesticides or herbicides and growth hormones or antibiotics. The market provides one of the few local places to get grass-fed beef. The body care and cleaning products are all natural and as local and organic as it gets. Try the roll-on body butter in vanilla or patchouli scents. We promise you will love your

visit to Sweetwater. Hackley Health at the Lakes, Harvey Street just a half of a mile South of Lakes Mall. Exit US 31 at Pontaluna Road. The market is held in the parking lot in summer and fall and inside the lobby in winter and during inclement weather. (231) 893-3937. www.sweetwaterlocal-foodsmarket.org

ANTIQUES

Airport Antique Mall
Here you'll find several dealers under one roof—antiques, collectibles, furniture, jewelry and more. 4206 Grand Haven Road, across from Cinema Carousel. Monday through Saturday 11:00 a.m. to 5:30 p.m., Sundays 12:00 noon to 5:30 p.m.

Muskegon Antique Mall
Off the beaten path, but well worth the excursion, the Antique Mall features a fine selection of Bakelite, beautiful furniture and something old for every taste. Located off of US 31 between Muskegon and Grand Haven. 5905 Old Grand Haven Road. Monday through Saturday 11:00 a.m. to 6:00 p.m., Sunday 1:00 p.m. to 6:00 p.m. (231) 798-6441. www.muskegonantiquemall.com

Bienvenue Antiques
A unique antique shopping experience in a turn-of-the-20th-century house, this collection features art and apparel. Open Fridays and Saturdays. 124 S. Mears Avenue, Whitehall. (231) 894-6856.

MALL COUNTRY

The Lakes Mall
The Lakes Mall stores draw in many visitors to the area as well as locals. The mall has such familiar national names as The Gap, American Eagle, Buckle, Bed, Bath and Beyond, Bath and Body Works, Christopher & Banks, Claire's, C.J. Banks, Dick's Sporting Goods and Hollister Co. There are also footwear shops like Journeys, Footlocker, Finish Line, Payless ShoeSource, Shoe Dept. and Tradehome Shoes. Department stores include JC Pennys, Sears and Younkers. The food court offers Chinese, smoothies, pizza, and more.

Mall hours are Monday through Saturday 10:00 a.m. to 9:00 p.m. and Sunday 11:00 a.m. to 6:00 p.m. Gift certificates are available. 5600 Harvey Street. (231) 798-7154. www.thelakesmall.com

Lakeshore Marketplace
After leaving the Lakes Mall, you might head over to Lakeshore Marketplace for open-air shopping in more national department and specialty stores, including Target, Old Navy, TJ Maxx, Barnes & Noble and Hobby Lobby. Hours vary. 5241 Harvey . (231) 798-3261.

Dine Out
The Lakes Mall area offers a wide variety of dining choices. Enjoy delicious dishes at familiar chain and independent restaurants such as Olive Garden, Red Lobster, Johnny Carrino's, Buffalo Wild Wings, Brann's, Perkin's, Famous India and more.

OTHER SHOPPING

Lee & Birch
Don't miss this one-stop boutique for modern-contemporary clothing and household items. One of a kind for Muskegon! Features friendly staff and unique apparel, shoes and accessories from Free People, Tulle, AG Jeans, BCBG Girls, French Connection and more. 255 Seminole. (231) 733-7500.

Photo Shops
At a time when you can buy an inexpensive digital camera just about anywhere, Muskegon is fortunate to have two full-service photo equipment stores that still deal in film. Both have a long tradition of excellent customer service. For photo processing, new cameras and helpful technicians, try **Radium Photo** downtown at 835 Terrace Avenue. (231) 726-3803. The **Camera Store** is an excellent resource for your film and video needs. 2634 Henry Street. (231) 733-1286.

Wasserman's Floral
Serving the Muskegon community for over 125 years, Wasserman is one of the city's oldest commercial establishments. Stop and smell the roses, and you'll quickly see why. 1595 Lakeshore Drive. (800) 730-2112.

Wayne's Deli and Beverage
Family-owned and operated for over 50 years, Wayne's Deli attracts their customers with a variety of specialty wines, coffees, microbrew beers, and foods. Lunch time also brings in people to eat a tasty assortment of gourmet sandwiches. This is also the place to create your own gift baskets. 746 W. Laketon Avenue. (231) 722-6833. www.waynesdeli.com

Muskegon Mercantile

Operated by and located in the Muskegon County Museum, the Mercantile is the place to find local history books, including titles like *Romance of Muskegon* and *Looking Aft*. Michigan-themed souvenirs like Petoskey stones, artwork, cards and a mourning dove pin based on a Hackley House carving are also available here. 430 West Clay Street. (231) 722-0278.

McDonalds Homemade Candies and Coffee Shop

Sold at shops around town, McDonalds Homemade Candies is headquartered in a corner store that's a magnet for the sweet tooth crowd. A perfect place to bring the kids, McDonalds is known for its sponge candy, chocolate covered pretzels and seafoam. 1064 South Getty Street. (231) 773-0319.

BOOKSTORES

Muskegon has four full-service bookstores ranging from "big box" to cozy neighborhood establishments where you can spend the afternoon browsing among good books.

North Shore Books

North Shore Books is a great place to find new and used books, enjoy coffee or tea, and find a wireless connection. If you're working on a new project, be sure to ask about manuscript indexing and editing. Now that's what we call full service. 315 Center Street, North Muskegon. (231) 670-7113. www.northshorebookstore.com

Book Nook and Java Shop
Book House and Java Shoppe is the place to go for new books, live entertainment, author events and reading groups. Coffee, pastries and the Internet make this establishment a local favorite. Visiting authors have included Diane Rehm and Garrison Keillor. 8726 Ferry Street, Montague, MI 49437. (231) 894-5333. www.thebooknookjavashop.com

Barnes & Noble
Barnes & Noble offers a wide selection of discounted books as well as a local interest section and general trade books and magazines. A popular coffee bar and author events make this mall location a popular stop. 5275 Harvey Street. (231) 798-4388.

Family Christian Bookstore
Family Christian Bookstore is the place to go for religious books, bibles, videos and gifts. 5506 Harvey Street. (231) 798-0024. www.familychristian.com

GALLERIES

Art Cats Gallery
Brighten up your day with a visit to this gallery featuring over 40 artists. Unique jewelry, fun and functional pottery, kiln fired and blown glass, furniture, sculpture and more. A great place to find American craft items, this eclectic gallery is open year-round. Owner Louise Hopson's mirrors, mosaics, bowls and teapots are functional work with a whimsical touch. 1845 Lakeshore Drive, Lakeside. (231) 755-7606. www.artcatsgallery.com. A Muskegon Best Bet.

Clay Avenue Cellars

A winery and gallery in one, this downtown Muskegon gem exhibits and sells the works of over 30 local artists. Art pieces include watercolors, oil paintings, photographs, pottery, jewelry, sculpture, fused and stained glass and more. 611 Clay Avenue. (231) 722-3108. www.clayavenue cellars.com

Claybanks Pottery

Watch as clay artists throw functional and raku pottery. The shop offers one of the most extensive collections of wheel-thrown pottery—cups, dishes, lamps and more. May through November. 7060 South Scenic Drive, New Era. (231) 894-4177.

Jilly's Gallery

Satisfy your whims with Jilly's collection of handmade porcelain ornaments and figures, as well as fused dichroic glass jewelry, driftwood creations and wall pieces. 471 W. Western. (231) 728-1515.

Through the Looking Glass

This art gallery, studio and gift boutique exhibits paintings, photography, sculpture and more from West Michigan artists. 1812 Lakeshore Drive. (231) 282-1152.

Wishes & Watercolors

One-of-a-kind Lake Michigan-themed gifts include hand-painted greeting cards, note cards, magnets and water-colors by owner and artist Karen Fethke. 1853 Ruddiman Drive. (231) 719-1231. www.wishesandwatercolors.com

OUTDOOR NEEDS

Go Gear Outdoors

Providing gear for the outdoors while specializing in hiking and backpacking, Go Gear also has a large selection of footwear and apparel. The store offers gear for all skill levels. Apparel and footwear brands include The North Face, Ex-Officio, Royal Robbins, Watergirl, Marmot, Teva, Keen, Merrill, and Mountain Hardwear. Go Gear is located near the Lakes Mall. 5141 Harvey Street. (231) 799-8788. www.gogearoutdoors. com

Powers Outdoors

Rugged gear, kayaks, and brand-name clothing and shoes fill this shop for people seeking new adventures. Clothing and shoe brands include Columbia Sportswear, Marmot, The North Face, Teva, Keen, Life is Good and many more. Visitors can check out the selection of kayaks and canoes and learn about upcoming events such as the Powers Outdoors annual kayak symposium. Also available here is a wide range of camping gear including tents, sleeping bags, and backpacks. 4523 Dowling Street, Montague. (231) 893-0687. http://www.powersoutdoors.com

West Marine

Another good place to shop for nautical supplies from wetsuits to water skis, fishing equipment and outdoor wear is West Marine. 2492 Henry Street #B. (231) 759-7709. www. westmarine.com

RESTAURANT GUIDE

Muskegon's restaurant scene has changed dramatically in recent years. In the heart of a major farming region, the community's restaurant culture benefits from a wide array of local fruits and vegetables, seafood, beef and poultry. From Michigan wines to locally caught salmon, you can expect to find regional ingredients on every menu. While western Michigan is well known for its cherries, blueberries, strawberries and apples, many first-time visitors are surprised to discover other local favorites such as artisan cheese, morel mushrooms, walleye and whitefish. (Alas, most of the ever-popular perch actually hails from Canada.) Don't let modest surroundings or low prices put you off. Good cooking and good values abound in a city that continues to attract talented chefs. In 2009, Baker College will open the Michigan Culinary Institute downtown, assuring a steady supply of talented new chefs. The institute will have a restaurant and bakery open to the public. Here are some restaurants worthy of consideration in all price ranges. Look for updated listings at www.rdrbooks.com/Muskegon

COFFEE AND TEA TIME

From mocha to mint tea, it's easy to find a place to settle in, sip a beverage, order a pastry, a bagel or a corned beef sandwich, enjoy the paper or catch up on your e-mail. While these establishments vary, all are good bets for takeout.

Brooklyn Bagels
A wide array of coffee drinks, tea and a variety of sodas complement an extensive breakfast and lunch menu. There's wireless Internet for customers' use. 475 Whitehall Road, North Muskegon. (213) 719-1623 and 3009 Henry, Roosevelt Park. (231) 733-1946.

Starbucks
Starbucks is always a reliable bet if you need a caffeine break while making the mall rounds. Wireless. 5840 Harvey Street, at the Lakes Mall. (231) 798-9787.

Goodgrains Bake House
A local favorite. Be sure to give the turtle brownies a try. Great soups and sandwiches and a handy outdoor patio make Good Grains a good lunch choice. 991 West Broadway, Roosevelt Park. (231) 759-4545.

Great Lakes Java Co.
There's a convenient takeout location at 2347 Sherman Boulevard. (231) 755-9896.

The Coffee House
This comfortable, cozy location features a full line of coffee drinks and smoothies, sandwiches and generous deserts. Fireplace seating makes this bright, well-lit establishment a popular gathering spot. On the Business US 31 corridor near Mona Lake. 255 Seminole Road. (231) 733-5535.

GREAT VIEWS

One of the great things about dining out in Muskegon is that you really can. During the warm months there are many choices with marine views and patio dining, accompanied at times by live music. Here are a few good choices:

Dockers Fish House and Lounge
One of the best patios in town. Covered in our restaurant section below, this is a great place to come to enjoy views of Muskegon Lake, channel boat traffic and the adjacent yacht harbor. Enjoy live music on summer weekends. Moderate to expensive. 3505 Marina View Point. (231) 755-0400.

Lakeside Inn
This historic property overlooking White Lake is another good choice if you like to watch the catamarans, kayaks and Jet Skis while enjoying a beer or a glass of wine. A perfect setting for a casual get-together. Moderate to expensive. 5700 N. Scenic Drive, Whitehall. (231) 893-8315.

Main Street Pub & Eatery
Overlooking Muskegon Lake, Main Street is a wise choice for a drink. With new management, expect an expanded menu that includes burgers, perch sandwiches, a salad bar and, of course, a full bar menu. Perfect for sunset dining. Moderate. 1113 Ruddiman Drive. (231) 744-7139.

Michillinda Lodge
Come to this perfect garden setting for a drink at sunset. This establishment in one of the region's most popular resorts has a great patio and easy access to the beach below. It's ideal for a summer gathering. Moderate to expensive. 5207 Scenic Drive, Whitehall. (231) 893-1895.

Rafferty's
The perfect waterfront location, come for a drink, enjoy the sunset and order one of the featured entrees such as garlic shrimp pasta, barbecued pork ribs or lake perch. Deck dining is popular in the summer months. Moderate to expensive. 730 Terrace Point. (616) 722-4461.

GREAT EATS

Select your preference from Muskegon's plethora of fast and fine dining options—you won't be disappointed.

750 Grill
A sleeper on the Northside, the 750 Grill offers gourmet pizzas with regular or whole wheat crusts, first-rate sandwiches and macaroni and cheese, along with a handsome bar, outdoor seating and prompt service. This smoke-free

establishment is priced right for the whole family. Moderate. 2190 Whitehall Road, Northside. (231) 744-7507.

Bellacino's
Gourmet sandwiches, subs and pizza make this eatery ideal for a quick lunch or a picnic gathering. A step up from Subway, Bellacino's will satisfy the pickiest eater. A great takeout or dine-in location close to US 31. Inexpensive. 1871 Holton Road, Suite B, Northside. (231) 744-3111.

Bernie O's
Sure, it's not the cheapest pizza in town, but if you're maxed out on pepperoni specials, stop in to try The Twist, a national winner in the *Pizza Today Magazine* competition. This house specialty features honey mustard, breaded chicken chunks and bacon strips. After baking, the chef tops your order with pineapple, tomato, peppers and ranch dressing. Other specialties include cherry pesto, Greek artichoke and the popular hot wing pizza. You'll also find subs and salads at this handy restaurant next door to North Shore Books. Inexpensive to moderate. 321 Center Street, North Muskegon. (231) 744-4900. www.bernieos.com

Brownstone
Quick service for passengers headed out on a flight, this Muskegon County Airport establishment also has pastas, seafood, gourmet sandwiches, soups and excellent desserts. A meeting room is perfect for small gatherings. Moderate. 101 Sinclair Drive. (231) 798-2273.

C.F. Prime Chophouse & Wine Bar
Muskegon's top steak house with prices to match, this intimate restaurant is the place for prime rib, seafood, chicken,
veal and pasta. An elegant setting and bar make C.F. Prime
a busy, smoke-free venue. Come hungry and you'll have
room for lavish desserts. Moderate to expensive. 950 West
Roosevelt Park. (231) 737-4943. A Muskegon Best Bet.

Carmen's Café and Mercantile
Carmen's is a popular downtown breakfast and lunch establishment known for its open-face steak sandwich, burgers,
triple-decker clubs, soups and antipasto salads. A roomy
new location makes Carmen's a great gathering place and
a good bet for take-out. Bring the kids. Free wireless. 878
Jefferson. (231) 726-6317.

Cherokee Restaurant
One of Muskegon's busiest breakfast establishments is also a
good bet for lunch and, on some nights, dinner. The Cherokee is known for its blueberry pancakes, waffles, omelettes
and cinnamon rolls. Smoke-free, this restaurant is ideal for
family gatherings and can handle big groups. Inexpensive.
1971 W. Sherman Boulevard, Roosevelt Park. (231) 759-7006.

City Café
Located in the basement of the Frauenthal Theater, the City
Café is perfect prelude to a symphony or theater at the adjacent Beardsley Theater. Gourmet soups and salads, seafood
entrees and a variety of pasta dishes, as well as steaks and
poultry are complimented by a full bar. Moderate. 411 W.
Western Avenue. (231) 725-7769.

Coastline Deli

A memorable view of Muskegon Lake and much of the city is found at Coastline Deli on the seventh floor of Terrace Plaza downtown. Open at 9:00 a.m. for coffee and pastries, Coastline serves a variety of soups, salads, and sandwiches along with specialty coffees at lunchtime. Panoramic views make this a great place to enjoy a lumberjack stacked roast beef sandwich on eight-grain bread, a California Reuben or the vegetarian Milwaukee Clipper. Inexpensive to moderate. 316 Morris Street. (231) 722-6106.

Dockers Fish House and Lounge

One of the city's favorite seafood establishments also offers gourmet hamburgers, pasta specialties, steaks and an impressive dessert menu. A full bar, outdoor seating, weekend bands in the summer and the best waterfront location in town make Dockers a perennial favorite for the boating crowd as well as landlubbers. There really is a dock where you can tie up your yacht or kayak. Moderate to expensive. 3505 Marina View Point. (231) 755-0400.

El Tapatio

Setting the standard for Mexican cuisine, El Tapatio's from-scratch cooking has made it a favorite with fans who love the food and the prices, particularly on Tuesdays and Thursdays when tacos go for just $1. Its modest but spotless dining room offers first rate chicken enchiladas, shrimp fajitas, chile rellenos and one of the best pico de gallos in the state, even though it's not on the menu. Let your waiter know if you prefer spicy entrees, as this establishment cooks on the mild side. Takeout and free delivery. Inexpensive. 1026 West Laketon Avenue. (231) 759-7408. A Muskegon Best Bet.

Fricanos
Founded in Grand Haven, Fricanos is the region's oldest pizza chain. Its thin-crust pizzas are inexpensive and served with or without anchovies. Fricano's Muskegon offers half-baked take-out pizzas, a full bar and a convenient location on the west side of downtown. Inexpensive. 1050 W. Western. (231) 722-7775.

Glenside Pub
A popular lunch, dinner and drinking spot, this is the place for burgers, nachos, sandwiches and some of the best pizzas in town. The Glenside attracts a mixed crowd that is typically in a celebratory mood. Inexpensive. 1508 Sherman Boulevard. (231) 759-8525.

Glenside Café
A popular breakfast and lunch spot, this modest establishment features fast service, generous portions and modest prices. The omelets, burgers and perch sandwiches are recommended. Inexpensive. 1125 West Hackley Avenue. (231) 755-8448.

Grand Traverse Pie Company
Sandwiches, pot pies, cherry pies, muffins, and coffee drinks make Grand Traverse a good lunch choice, known for its quick service and take-home pies. Inexpensive. 5817 Harvey Street, near the Lakes Mall. (231) 799-3399.

Harbor Steakhouse
Located in the Holiday Inn, the Harbor offers a breakfast buffet and an eclectic lunch and dinner menu with a focus on beef, seafood and pasta. The Harbor is also a good

place for a drink after an event at the Frauenthal Theater or a Fury game at the Walker Arena. Moderate to expensive. 939 Third Street. (231) 720-7123.

Hearthstone Restaurant

An extensive menu ranging from croque monsieur sandwiches to panko-encrusted walleye specials help make the Hearthstone Muskegon's favorite bistro. A great place for a business lunch or a birthday celebration, the Hearthstone's full bar, extensive wine list and fireplace add to the fun. Don't miss the flatbread specials, hearty soups or the bread pudding. For a late night dessert or a steak dinner, this restaurant is across the street from Meijer's and about as far as you can get from the chain gang. Moderate to expensive. 3350 Glade Street. (231) 733-1056. A Muskegon Best Bet.

Hobo's Tavern

A welcome addition on the northside, Hobo's is a good choice for hamburgers, sandwiches, pasta, seafood and steaks. A handsome bar and summertime patio seating make Hobo's a popular gathering spot. Come for lunch or a nightcap and you'll enjoy the service and the reasonable prices. Moderate. 1411 Whitehall Road, North Muskegon. (231) 719-0247.

Mango's

Jimmy Buffet tunes piped out over a snowbound parking lot put you in a parrothead mood for Mango's, a Caribbean-style eatery and bar that is strong on panini, perch and margaritas. Mexican dishes, seafood and sandwiches are all served efficiently at this friendly establishment, where you'll also find live music on weekends. Moderate. 1811 West Sherman Boulevard.

Mike's Landing

A popular breakfast and lunch spot, Mike's is a moderately priced café with a focus on omelettes, burgers, sandwiches and Mexican fare. Quick service and a handy takeout menu. Inexpensive. 1384 West Laketon Avenue. (231) 755-8600.

Mr. B's Pancake House

You'll enjoy this popular breakfast and lunch establishment with its menu featuring cherry pancakes, a Southwest chicken wrap and ribeye steaks. Inexpensive to moderate. 1437 Whitehall Road, North Muskegon. (231) 719-2337.

Pints & Quarts

Patio seating in the summer months and a lounge style dining area make Pints & Quarts one of the city's leading pubs. The focus is on crispy calamari, stacked Reubens, Cobb salads and seared salmon. An impressive list of beers ranging from imports to regional microbrews as well as a great wine list adds to the celebratory atmosphere. Pints & Quarts is the place to be seen and heard. Moderate. 950 West Norton, Roosevelt Park. (231) 830-9889.

The Pita Place

When it comes to fast Middle Eastern and Greek food, there's no need to lower your expectations. Whether you dine in or go for the drive-through, count on first-rate pitas, gyros, and falafel as well as a variety of soups. Inexpensive. 2039 East Apple Avenue. (231) 773-7482.

Racquets Downtown Grill

A popular sports bar that's strong on burgers, sandwiches and salads, Racquets is a good bet for pre-Fury game dining downtown. Feel free to reach for a beer if e-mail coming in on the free wireless connection is getting to you. The late night pub atmosphere makes Racquets a perennial favorite with sports couch potatoes. Moderate. 446 West Western Avenue. (231) 726-4007.

Ryke's Bakery and Café

From burritos, chowders and stews to chocolate cake, Ryke's is a great place to pick up a cup of espresso, check your e-mail or place a takeout sandwich order. A Muskegon landmark, you'll enjoy the friendly service and from-scratch cooking. Inexpensive. 1788 Terrace. (231) 726-2253.

Sam's Bistro

The place for Mediterranean food, Sam's offers patio dining during the summer. Falafel, Fattoush salads, eggplant dishes, chicken kabob and Middle Eastern pizzas are served at a relaxed pace. Moderate. 306 East Colby Street, Whitehall. (231) 893-3000. A Muskegon Best Bet.

Sardine Room

Intimate fireside dining, an excellent wine list, attentive service and one of the city's better menus make this small restaurant a local favorite. From salmon pasta to fajitas, everything is a good value. Black Angus beef burgers, Reuben sandwiches, entrée salads and Jack Daniels salmon are all well prepared. Enjoy the small patio in warm weather. Moderate to expensive. 2536 Henry Street. (231) 755-5008. A Muskegon Best Bet.

Station Grill

A gas station reincarnated as a burger joint heavy on automotive décor, the Station is also a good bet for salads, sandwiches and chili. In addition to an extensive list of half-pound burgers, the menu offers chicken and turkey sandwiches and, for those who are not worried about their cholesterol, parmesan cheese fries. Moderate. 910 W. Broadway. (231)759-0633. A Muskegon Best Bet.

Steak N Egger
Come early or be prepared to wait for this café that serves excellent omelettes, blueberry pancakes, French toast and other breakfast specialties to a loyal crowd. The lunch menu is also a hit, with a focus on burgers, soups, chili and roast beef sandwiches. Inexpensive. 1535 Holton Road (M-120), Northside. (231) 719-8939.

Toast 'n Jam's Restaurant
A bright sunlit dining room makes this cheery breakfast and lunch establishment a busy place. Omelettes, pancakes, Belgian waffles, sourdough French toast, cinnamon rolls, eggs Benedict and quiche are all popular. For lunch, try the beer-battered halibut sandwich or the guiltless panini. Moderate. 5550 Henry Street. (231) 737-5267.

Tony's Bistro
A longtime favorite now at home in a larger dining room on Business US 31, Tony's is the place to go for good steak, seafood or pasta dishes. The southern Mediterranean and Greek cooking includes oven fired pizza. A popular choice for a family night out, Tony's is also a good bet for a romantic dinner or a nightcap. Moderate to expensive. 212 Seaway Drive. (231) 739-7196.

US-31 BBQ
Pork, beef and chicken barbecue served at moderate prices have made this spot a community landmark. Not a ribs joint, US-31 specializes in sliced meat sandwiches. Inexpensive. 151 W. Muskegon Avenue, with a second location at 604 E. Colby in Whitehall. (231) 722-3948.

Wayne's Deli and Beverage
Family-owned and operated for over 50 years, Wayne's Deli is the place to find specialty wines like Beaujolais Nouveau, microbrews, house roasted coffee (try the Michigan cherry blend) and one of the biggest and best sandwich menus in town. Lunch time is prime time at the sandwich counter, where you can pick up a hoagie or design your own complete with gourmet cheeses and seven-grain bread. Inexpensive. 746 West Laketon Avenue. (231) 722-6833.

WEST MICHIGAN STRONGHOLDS

If you're new to the region, you'll certainly notice regional chains that have a strong local following. Here are four you'll want to consider checking out during your stay.

G & L Chili Dogs
With convenient locations around town, G & L has been whetting local appetites since 1926. This popular family establishment is a hit with the kids. In addition to its famous chili dogs, the restaurant also offers soups, sandwiches and shakes at budget prices. Inexpensive.

Meijers

It's hard to imagine any retailer outselling Wal-Mart, but that's the case when it comes to Meijers. Now found throughout the Midwest, this chain developed by Frederik Meijer originated the superstore concept. It's a modern version of the general store. Based in Walker, the chain has three locations in North Muskegon, Norton Shores and across from the Lakes Mall. www.meijers.com.

Plumb's

This local grocery chain with stores in Muskegon, Muskegon Heights, Norton Shores, North Muskegon and Whitehall is a handy place to stop with fast, friendly service and a good selection. Easy-to-navigate stores are a good bet for customers who value their time and appreciate the focus on food in a non-superstore environment. Plumb's is also known for its support of community events. www.plumbsmarket.com

Wesco

It's hard to go anywhere in the Muskegon area without passing a Wesco. At this competitively priced gas station and convenience store, you can get a *New York Times*, coffee, a lottery ticket and a wide selection of donuts. www.gowesco.com

LOCAL FAVORITES

Muskegon has a lot of traditional favorites with loyal clientele such as the US-31 BBBQ and the House of Chan. Here are more places locals enjoy.

Dog 'N Suds

This traditional drive-in, featuring frosty root beer mugs, cheeseburgers, pork tenderloin, shrimp baskets, onion rings and veggie platters, has been in business for over 40 years. Car hops are all part of the fun. The establishment has been highlighted on the *Today Show*. Inexpensive. 4454 Dowling, Montague, (231) 894-4991; and 4221 Grand Haven Road, (231) 798-4976.

El Camino Taco

A south-of-the-border Muskegon landmark with budget Mexican dining, El Camino is the place for guacamole salads, chicken picadillo, fajitas and quesadillas. Inexpensive. Open 'til midnight Monday through Thursday. 785 W. Broadway. (231) 739-7833.

Frosty Oasis

Be prepared to stand in line and make new friends on warm summer nights here in the heartland of dairy delights like awesome turtle sundaes, grasshoppers, root beer floats and giant dipped soft-serve cones. This is the place where teens, truck drivers, CEOs and ministers meet to eat. Inexpensive. 2181 Sherman. (231) 755-2903.

House of Chan/Joe's Steak House

A Muskegon institution, House of Chan now shares space with Joe's Steak House. An extensive and moderately priced buffet is the prime attraction, but you can also opt for sirloin, burgers or the heart healthy menu. Moderate. 375 Gin Chan Avenue. (231) 733-9624.

Pablo's

Another bargain Mexican restaurant with a local following. Burritos, tacos, enchiladas and salads are all popular here with loyal patrons who consider this establishment a culinary second home. Inexpensive. 1427 Sherman. (231) 759-8400.

Ruth Ann's Ice Cream

A great summertime stop at Muskegon State Park and the perfect respite on a bike ride up Scenic Drive, this is the place for smoothies, sundaes, hot fudge cream puffs, or a flurry. Inexpensive. 605 Scenic Drive, North Muskegon. (231) 744-8775.

Whippy Dip

A popular ice cream stand, Whippy Dip is a place where you best forget about calorie-counting. Indulge yourself in a hot fudge sundae, a thick strawberry malt or a banana split. Enjoy today, diet tomorrow. 977 East Pontaluna Road, Spring Lake on the way to Hoffmaster Park. (231) 798-2280 or Whippy Dip North at 1326 Holton Road. (231) 744-2723.

SMOKE-FREE RESTAURANTS

Muskegon is not smoke-free, but if you're looking for a smoke-free restaurant, you have a long list of choices that continues to grow. For a quick reference guide, go to www.mchp.org or call (231) 728-3201. A handy brochure is also available from the Muskegon Community Health Project at 565 Western Avenue. In spring 2008, the Michigan State Senate passed a no-smoking law that went on to the Michigan House of Representatives. This could lead to a permanent smoking ban in restaurants statewide.

WHITE LAKE AREA

Whitehall and Montague, the small towns rimming White Lake, have long been popular summer resorts. Major destinations such as Michillinda Lodge and the Lakeside Inn are venerable family favorites. Scenic drives, relaxing beaches, marinas, art galleries, bed and breakfasts, canoe trips, an old fashioned soda fountain, first-class community theater and easy access to some of the region's best known resorts make this area a must for any Muskegon area visitor. This area is also a good year-round destination thanks to bargain off-season pricing. From spring bike tours to ringing in the New Year at a bed and breakfast retreat, the White Lake area offers a relaxing alternative to higher priced resorts. For more information, contact the White Lake Area Chamber of Commerce, 124 Hanson Street, Whitehall. (231) 893-4585 or www.whitelake.org. Also highly recommended is the

White Lake Community Library. An excellent regional resource, this is a great place to learn more about the region and bring the kids for story time. 3900 White Lake Drive, Whitehall. (231) 894-9531. www.whitelake.llcoop.org

White River Light Station
Climb to the top of the light station via a spiral staircase to enjoy panoramic views of Lake Michigan and White Lake. This brick and limestone lighthouse was built in 1875 and now houses a maritime museum. Exhibits include a ship's helm, fog horn and navigation instruments. You'll also learn about the steamship *Carolina*, which provided scheduled service to Chicago. Open Memorial Day to Labor Day and weekends in September. 6199 Murray Road, Whitehall. (231) 894-8265.

Medbury Park
On the tranquil Montague shoreline, this beach offers 600 feet of Lake Michigan frontage immediately north of White Lake Channel. The adjacent park has a volleyball court, quiet, shaded picnic areas and benches along the channel, a popular fishing spot. Near White River Light Station, Medbury Park offers easy access to the Hart-Montague Trail. 6:00 a.m. to 11:00 p.m. No lifeguard on duty. Lifeguard Road, Montague.

WHITE LAKE SHOPPING

Don't miss the unique collection of shops and galleries offered in the area. Here are some of the best.

Colby Street Shops Antique Mall

The place to go for art, antiques and collectibles, this small mall convenient to White Lake and the Howmet Playhouse features vintage comics, paintings, stained glass and memorabilia, 106 E. Colby, Whitehall. (231) 893-1369.

The Corner House of Gifts

An extensive collection of American arts and crafts and Christmas gifts fills the Corner House. Jewelry, vintage kitchenware and tableware are among the highlights here. 233 East Colby. (231) 893-5235. www.cornerhouseofgifts.com

Lipka's Old Fashioned Soda Fountain

Home of a 1946 Bastian Blessing fountain, Lipka's has been reborn thanks to the hard work of Patti Ream, daughter of founder Glen Lipka, who operated the shop for 50 years. Thanks to a new lunch room serving sandwiches, Lipka's now welcomes the next generation of regulars at the region's sole remaining soda fountain. Lipka's is home base for the October Pumpkinfest's main event, a pumpkin weigh-in. It's also a great spot to watch the pumpkin roll where you can have a chance to send your own carefully picked pumpkin rolling down Dowling Hill. 8718 Ferry Street, Montague. (231) 893-5624.

Klinefelter's Gallery

Regional artwork portraying Lake Michigan, dunes and lighthouses is the heart of this popular White Lake gallery. 1124 Mears, Whitehall. (231) 893-0194.

White River Gallery
This cooperative gallery features regional artists with a mixed media focus. Exhibitions highlight paintings, textiles, ceramics and sculpture. 8701 Ferry, Montague. (231) 894-8659.

The Nuveen Center for the Arts
Adjacent to the White River Gallery, the Nuveen Center for the Arts offers art workshops and classes for adults and children, as well as exhibitions of work by local and regional artists. 8697 Ferry, Montague. (231) 894-2787.

Page's
Brand name furniture, collectibles, handmade jewelry and stained-glass supplies are featured here along with classes that teach dichroic jewelry making. 4574 Dowling, Montague. (231) 894-5688.

The Paisley Place
When it's time for tea and biscuits, stop on by this wood paneled retreat, which also features handsome gifts. An elegant setting makes Paisley Place a local favorite. Call ahead to confirm lunch and tea times. Private parties by arrangement. 4578 Dowling, Montague. (231) 893-4832.

Pitkins Drug and Gift Shoppe
Distinctive gifts are a major draw at this shop, which has been serving White Lake area customers for 125 years. Pitkins offers one-stop shopping for souvenirs, beachwear and cottage decor. This is the place to go for White Lake T-shirts. 107 West Colby, Whitehall. (231) 893-5495.

Utopian Marketplace
The Utopian Marketplace focuses on natural foods, grass-fed beef and free-range chicken, organic dairy products, nutritional supplements, wheat- and gluten-free products, locally-grown organic vegetables and salads. A small juice bar and sandwich shop, books focusing on health and nutrition and music are also found here. This is the only place in the Muskegon area where you can find wheatgrass shots. 8832 Water, Montague. (231) 894-9530.

GREENHOUSES AND NURSERIES

The White Lake area boasts a seasonal assortment of fruits, vegetables and plants, ideal souvenirs for green thumbs and master gardeners alike. Check out one of the region's quality nurseries to gather this year's crop.

Weesies Brothers Farms, Inc.
Growing in the White Lake area since 1910, Weesies Brothers Farms, is headquartered in Montague. The garden centers sell annuals, perennials, rose bushes, trees, shrubs, and vegetables. 10126 Walsh Road, Montague. (231) 894-4742.

White Lake Greenhouse
A good choice for fresh flowers, tropicals and house plants, White Lake Greenhouse also features a broad gift line. 703 East Colby Street, Whitehall. (231) 894-9011.

Barry's Flower Shop and Greenhouses
Barry's 14 greenhouses offer blooming shrubs, trees and plants. The flower shop specializes in silk and dried arrangements as well as wreaths and swags. 3000 Whitehall Road, North Muskegon. (231) 766-3031.

WEDDINGS

Coming to Muskegon and you wanna get married? There are lots of great locations here. The tough part will be choosing, but you have to start making decisions somewhere so let's look at the basics first: indoors or outdoors?

Sites for indoor weddings include churches, bed and breakfasts and inns, clubs, a boat, restaurants and halls, and other facilities. Here are some to consider:

CHURCHES

There seem to be more churches per square mile in Muskegon than most towns, and they come in every flavor from Greek Orthodox to Baha'i. As someone said to me once, "There's a choice for everybody here, so everybody in Muskegon oughta be saved."

If you aren't affiliated with a Muskegon County house of worship but want a religious ceremony, start calling churches as far in advance as possible. In order to be married in a particular church, there can be membership requirements for you or your partner or both of you, or a family relationship with a church member may be required, or a church can limit those it will marry to couples who have attended counseling sessions with clergy or premarital group discussions or classes.

Theological matters aside however, depending on the size and the theme of your wedding, here are a variety of particularly cool churches to check out:

St. Paul's Episcopal Church
Dark wood, soaring ceilings, a good organ and beautiful windows impart a feeling that you've been transported somehow to England. There's a nice Guild Hall for merrily elegant receptions, and everything is handicapped accessible. A chapel is also available. 1006 Third Street in downtown Muskegon. (231) 722-2112.

St. Jean Baptiste Catholic Church
This beautiful old Roman Catholic church, with its warm white walls, gold trim, and glowing blue and multicolored windows with French inscriptions, was started by Muskegon's first French settlers. Originally French-speaking, masses are now said in Spanish. 1292 Jefferson Street. (231) 722-2793.

Central United Methodist Church
This cathedral has amazing high ceilings, incredible restored windows, and the longest center aisle you'll find in town.

A great place for a wedding if you've always wanted to get married in a stone cathedral while wearing a gown with a really long train. It has a great organ and a nice social hall for receptions. A chapel is also available. 1011 Second Street at Webster Avenue in downtown Muskegon. (231) 722-6545.

St. Francis De Sales Catholic Church

Designed by internationally renowned architect Marcel Breuer, this classy, contemporary Roman Catholic cathedral is stunningly world class. It's worth checking out just to gape at the incredible architecture, even if you're not Catholic and even if you're not getting married. The ceilings soar 90 feet above you in a stark grandeur that is unmatched. 2929 McCracken Avenue. (231) 755-1953.

Forest Park Covenant Church

This big but friendly, casual and contemporary church has all the facilities from a social hall to a basketball court to a chapel, with lots of parking. This church can and does handle contemporary praise worship bands. 3815 Henry Street. (231) 780-4784.

Temple B'nai Israel

This warm, inviting reform synagogue, a handsome sanctuary downtown across the street from Hackley Park, features stunning contemporary décor. 391 W. Webster. (231) 722-2702.

First Congregational Church–United Church of Christ

A classic of New England simplicity, this traditional red brick building has a single spire and an unadorned, white interior. Not air conditioned, but handicapped accessible, it has a good organ and a nice social hall. 1201 Jefferson Street. (231) 726-3254.

Mt. Zion Church of God in Christ
The largest African American church in downtown Muskegon will surround you with golden warmth and tradition. There's a nice social hall in the basement too. 188 W. Muskegon Avenue. (231) 722-6765.

First Church of Christ Scientist
This incredibly beautiful facility seats 500 in gorgeous smooth-curved wooden pews and features Frank Lloyd Wright-inspired windows. Air conditioned but not handicapped accessible. 280 W. Muskegon Avenue at Third Street. (231) 722-7704.

Bethany Christian Reformed Church
This large, traditional protestant church has a good organ, a very nice social hall, and a very active congregation. 1105 Terrace. (231) 725-7325.

BED AND BREAKFAST INNS

Port City Victorian Inn
This lovely Victorian bed and breakfast can accommodate a very small wedding—maybe 10 people—in an antique-filled elegant parlor with a view of Muskegon Lake. 1259 Lakeshore Drive. (231) 759-0205.

Langeland House

Early 20th century decor and welcoming hosts greet you at this newly established bed and breakfast located right across the street from Happy Endings, one of the best places in town to get a wedding cake. It can accommodate 20 to 30 people. There's a nifty dining room for cake-and-punch receptions. 1337 Peck Street. (231) 728-9404.

A Finch Nest

Non-denominational and cross-cultural weddings are particularly welcome at this B-and-B, which can also provide a cleric and is suitable for ceremonies or small receptions. 415 S. Division Street, Whitehall. (231) 893-5323. www.afinch nest.com

RIGHT ON THE WATER

Port City Princess

Cruise Lake Michigan on your special day! Complete wedding and reception packages offering food, music and decor for as many as 150 can include a band or a D.J. as well as space for dancing. You can't get any closer to the water than this, the only big boat in Muskegon County that actually leaves the dock. 560 Mart Street at the Mart Dock. (231) 728-8387. www.portcityprincesscruises.com

LST 393

This restored naval vessel is one of only two landing ships that remain from the invasion of France on D-Day in World War II. Weddings spaces on deck or indoors are available.

A canopy for shade or shelter can be arranged. The cool evening breezes and the view of the water are fantastic, and it poses no problem to guests who may fear the water—the ship hasn't left the dock in decades. 560 Mart Street. (231) 722-4730. Available all year.

ALMOST ON THE WATER BUT STILL ON LAND

Harbour View Room at Harbour Town Yacht Club
You'll find a lovely view of the harbor in this very nice newer facility, which can accommodate larger groups and dancing. Catering is available. At Harbour Town Marina near the channel between Muskegon Lake and Lake Michigan. 3425 Fulton, Muskegon. (231) 728-1261 or htyclub@verizon. net. Open all year.

Lakeside Inn
This beloved old summer resort offers years of wedding experience and can provide the location, dining, accommodations or all three right on the shore of White Lake. 5700 N. Scenic Drive, Whitehall. (231) 8793-8315. www.lakesideinn.net

Weathervane Inn
On the water in Montague, this newer facility offers a traditional lakeside ambiance. 4527 Dowling, Montague. (231) 893-8931.

Michillinda Lodge
The fabulous view of Lake Michigan from the Michillinda Lodge perches atop the dune overlooking the water, mak-

ing this old-time summer resort quite special. The lovely restaurant offers a beautiful view no matter the weather and great sunsets all year. Scenic Drive at Michillinda Drive, Whitehall. (231) 893-1895.

CLUBS

Greater Muskegon Women's Club
With beautiful hardwood floors perfect for dancing and a small balcony for throwing the bouquet, the Women's Club has been the site for small proms and special social events for over 100 years. A lovely living room could accommodate a ceremony for up to 50 as well. BYO caterer. 280 West Webster Avenue at Second Street, next door to the Muskegon Museum of Art. (231) 725-9220.

Muskegon Country Club
If you know a member, there isn't a better view or a classier venue in Muskegon. A lovely outdoor deck, handicapped accessible, air conditioned, a liquor license, and a good chef all make the country club a great choice. 7801 Lakeshore Drive. (231) 755-3737.

Old Channel Trail Golf Course
There's a beautiful spot for weddings on a high bluff overlooking Lake Michigan. (231) 894-5076. www.OCTgolf.com

BANQUET FACILITIES AND HALLS

Muskegon has lots of banquet facilities and halls. Many of the halls are associated with fraternal organizations of all the usual stripes. Here are three particularly noteworthy facilities:

Above and Beyond
This elegant banquet facility for large or small groups at the Moss Ridge Golf Club offers good food, good service, a nice dance floor and lots of parking. Near Hoffmaster State Park, it's easy to find for out-of-towners. 513 W. Pontaluna Road. (231) 798-4591. www.above-beyond.com

Frauenthal Center
This historic center for the performing arts in the heart of downtown Muskegon also books special events, including weddings, receptions and rehearsal dinners. Dinner seating up to 250 can be accommodated, with hors d'oeuvre reception space for up to 500. Catering partnerships with Muskegon's best. 425 W. Webster. (231) 332-4103. www.frauenthal.info

Trillium Banquet and Catering
This new banquet hall features an elegant ballroom and even a gazebo. Complete wedding packages for up to 600 are available. Locals know it for the delicious food. 17246 Van Wagoner, Spring Lake. (616) 842-8260. www.trilllium-mi.com.

OUTDOOR WEDDINGS

There are lots of beautiful sites for outdoor weddings in Muskegon County. Here are a few favorite choices for those beautiful days (and nights):

Custer Park
A lovely gazebo overlooking Muskegon Lake is a popular site for weddings, sometimes even two per day. Local rental places have all the details you'll need for chairs and arrangements. On Ruddiman Avenue in North Muskegon. Call the City of North Muskegon at (231) 744-1621 for reservations. The city also operates the Walker Community Center at 1522 Ruddiman, right across the street, a convenient location for receptions and dancing into the wee hours (or if the weather turns damp).

Heritage Memorial Garden
A large gazebo and a lovely garden are recent welcome additions to downtown Muskegon. Cost is just a $150 donation to the Muskegon Zonta Club and an event insurance certificate for your big day. 545 W. Western Avenue (between Fifth and Sixth Streets). Call Pam at (231) 737-9341 ext. 101 daytimes or (231) 798-1756 evenings.

Monet Garden
This gorgeous small garden was developed by a dedicated group of volunteers from the Master Gardeners of Muskegon following the famous painting of Monet's garden at Giverny. Corner of Fifth Street and Clay Avenue. Contact the Muskegon County/MSU Cooperative Extension office at (231) 724-4730 for more information.

Heritage Landing

There's a lovely spot for a small wedding on the footbridge overlooking Muskegon Lake. The sun setting behind the bride and groom make a perfect picture. Shoreline Drive. Contact Muskegon County at (231) 724-6417 for Heritage Landing reservations.

ON THE MOVE

Muskegon Trolley Company

Celebrate the moment on a trolley! One trolley or several can transport you and your whole party from one location to another in restored self-propelled comfort. (231) 798-1546.

West Coast Carriage Company

This is the place to rent a horse-drawn carriage in the downtown Muskegon area. 557 W. Clay Avenue. (231) 855-2758.

COOL PLACES THAT DON'T ALLOW WEDDINGS

Don't bother to call. We won't give you their phone numbers. It ain't gonna happen.

Muskegon County Museum
Hackley & Hume Historic Site
Muskegon Museum of Art
Hackley Public Library
Torrent House

MICHIGAN'S ADVENTURE AND WILDWATER ADVENTURE

The largest theme park in the state bills itself as two playgrounds in one—Michigan's Adventure, with about 40 carnival-style rides, and WildWater Adventure, with more than a dozen slides, wave pools and other soaking-wet thrills. The two are actually part of the same park, under the same management and included in the same all-inclusive admission price, but the open hours are different, and the ride park has a slightly longer season than the water park. The biggest difference is dress codes: in the ride areas, shirts, shoes and shorts are required, and swimwear must be appropriately covered, but in the water park swimsuits are mandatory and regular shorts or T-shirts are not permitted. When going from one area to the other, you must stop in the locker rooms to change.

To beat long lines, try to get to the park before it opens to get in line for tickets. Wear light, breezy clothing, good walking shoes or water shoes, and stay hydrated in the heat with lots of water. Make sure to bring plenty of sunscreen and reapply throughout the day.

Admission to Michigan's Adventure and Wild Water Adventure is $25, and toddlers two years or younger get in free. Parking costs $8 per vehicle, and there is a $4 locker fee in the water park changing rooms. Two-day passes cost $44, and season passes are available for $89.95, plus $35 for a season parking pass. Michigan's Adventure opens in mid-May and operates until mid-September; WildWater Adventure opens the last weekend in May and operates until the first weekend in September. While park hours vary slightly from month to month, during the peak summer season the ride park is open daily from 11:00 a.m. to 9:00 p.m. (10:00 p.m. on Saturdays), and the water park is open daily from 12:00 noon to 7:00 p.m. 4750 Whitehall Road. (231) 766-3377. www.miadventure.com

MICHIGAN'S ADVENTURE

You'll get a spectacular view of the Muskegon area and the vastness of Lake Michigan from the top of the Giant Gondola Wheel. An equally impressive panorama can be glimpsed from the summit of the first hill on Shivering Timbers—but only briefly before the huge wooden roller coaster plunges its passengers into an ecstatically shrieking dive at 65 miles per hour.

The park got its start in 1956 as the Deer Park petting zoo. Over the next 45 years it evolved into a "two parks in one" carnival and water park attraction under local ownership. In 2001, Michigan's Adventure and WildWater Adventure were aquired by the same company that owns Cedar Point in Sandusky, Ohio, which has been named the "Best Amusement Park in the World" for each of 10 consecutive years by *Amusement Today* magazine, mostly because of its array of big roller coasters. In fact, the Muskegon park's box office sells season passes covering both Michigan's Adventure and Cedar Point (which are more than 200 miles apart) for $150.

Like Cedar Point, Michigan's Adventure offers one of the most exciting roller coaster collections you'll find anywhere. Besides the wooden Shivering Timbers—one of the world's largest roller coasters—there's the Wolverine Wildcat, the park's original wooden coaster, and the dramatic Corkscrew, which snaps riders through inverted rolls. And if that's not enough excitement, in 2008 the park premiered its fourth big roller coaster, the Thunderhawk, where passengers ride on seats suspended ski-lift-style from a steel track that twists, turns, and loops upside-down five times.

Besides the big coasters, Michigan's Adventure offers a host of other "high-thrill" rides that involve flying through the air at breakneck speed. For instance, the Mad Mouse careens through multiple levels of tight, fast turns. Then there are rides every amusement park buff will recognize: bumper cars, the Tilt-a-Whirl, the Trabant, the Sea Dragon, the Flying Trapeze, the Falling Star and, of course, the 50-foot-diameter carousel, a recent model that has classic saddle horses as well as more unusual carved animals, including a ridable chicken.

Other rides, while they are part of the ride park and not the water park for hours and dress code purposes, are intended to get you soaking wet. Logger's Run seats you in a hollow "log" and sends you down a chute of flowing water to splash down in a pool. Another "shoot-the-chute" ride, Adventure Falls, takes you up high, around, and then down under a bridge, soaking riders and passers-by alike. Grand Rapids takes passengers over simulated whitewater and under waterfalls in river rafts. The Hydroblaster waterslide lets you stay dry in a plastic raft or get as wet as you want. For something a little tamer, there's also a large, waveless manmade lake in the center of the park where kids and their parents can float around on swan-shaped pedal boats.

Michigan's Adventure is family-oriented above all, so it offers more rides for small children than many other amusement parks do. Most of them involve riding around in slow, gentle circles on tyke-sized cars, motorcycles, boats, airplanes, helicopters, elephants, whales and the like while parents catch a little rest on nearby benches. The Timbertown Railway, an authentic miniature steam train, carries young passengers around an open area with a pond, through a tunnel and along the bases of the two biggest roller coasters.

WILDWATER ADVENTURE

Considering the abundance of water sports opportunities to be found all over the Muskegon area, one may wonder why a commercial water park is not superfluous. The answer is *big thrills*. In fact, despite the amusement park's plethora of roller coasters, the water park actually boasts more "aggressive thrill rides"—the highest ride rating, not for the faint of heart. Are you ready to put your nerve to the test in a 300-foot enclosed tube that sends you whirling into a giant wet plastic cone and find out for yourself why they call it the Funnel of Fear?

There are five different pool areas, ranging from the Half-Pint Paradise, a wading pool with small slides and fountains, to several large wave pools including the seven-foot-deep Boogie Beach, where you'll find the biggest and most powerful waves. Bathers can also flow with the current on plastic tubes at the Lazy River, which winds through part of the water park. Whimsical, kid-friendly water playgrounds include Treehouse Harbor, with its short water slides, water cannons and a giant bucket that intermittently dumps torrents of water on those standing under it, and the Jolly Roger pirate ship.

Slides are the big thrills at any water park, and this one has no less than 13 of them. Some are body slides, while others are tube or raft slides. Some are fully enclosed, while others are wide open. Some feature sudden twists and turns like the wildest of roller coasters, while others shoot straight, steep and very fast. Names like the Cyclone Zone, the Wild Slide, the Slidewinder and the Snake Pit build adrenaline-pumping anticipation while waiting in line.

FOR A FEE

Michigan's Adventure features a few amusements and amenities that are not included in the park admission fee. Foremost among them is the Ripcord, which aficionados claim is so thrilling that even the roller coasters pale by comparison.

A nylon harness holds one to three passengers prone at the end of a flexible steel cable as they drop in a pendulum arc from a height of 183 feet, then soar like Superpeople back and forth over the park. Unlike bungee jumping, this thrill ride is more like flying than falling. Ripcord is not included in the main admission of Michigan's Adventure but has a hefty upcharge—more than the full cost of admission to the park and its other rides—because it can only carry one to three people at a time. The cost is $30 for one flyer, $40 for two flyers ($20 each) or for $45 for three flyers ($15 each).

For a smaller extra fee, visitors can drive gas-powered go-karts shaped like sleek, fast, red-white-and-blue miniature NASCAR racers at top speed around a track located beside the central manmade lake. Drivers (but not passengers) must be at least five feet tall and 12 years old (16 years old if carrying a passenger). The upcharge for a single driver is $5 for the first trip and $8 for each additional consecutive trip; a passenger pays $2 per trip. Kids too young or too short to qualify can drive slower cars at the smaller junior go-kart track, which is included in the main admission fee.

Rocky Point Mini-Golf, an 18-hole miniature golf course on a hilly island in the park's central manmade lake, offers family putting fun for a fee of $3 per person.

In the water park, you can rent one of 16 private, shady surfside tent cabanas with four lounge chairs and a table with four chairs. The cost is $60 for up to six people and another $5 apiece for up to two additional guests. Reservations are encouraged. (231) 766-9959.

SCHOOLS

Muskegon's public schools compete favorably with larger districts. Although all these districts have good academic programs, many of them are also known for their extracurricular activities. Muskegon High School's varsity football team has recorded sixteen state titles since 1920 and been rated #1 in the state by *Sports Illustrated*. At Mona Shores, an outstanding theater, choral and music program features groups like the Allegros and the Singing Christmas Tree at the Frauenthal Theater. Muskegon Heights marching band has traveled the world, and the school also has a great jazz band. Reeths Puffer has won three consecutive Michigan Competitive Bands Association State Championships. For the past six years, Montague has staged a Mock Rock concert to raise money for muscular dystrophy. North Muskegon High School is proud of the fact that 87 percent of its graduates go on to higher education. For more information on these and other high schools in the local community, contact:

Michigan Training and Education Center: 571 Apple Avenue. (231) 720-2530.

Muskegon High School: 80 W. Southern Avenue. (231) 720-2800. www.muskegon.k12.mi.us

Mona Shores High School: 1121 Seminole Road, Norton Shores. (231) 780-4711. www.monashores.net

Muskegon Heights High School: 2441 Sanford Street, Muskegon Heights. (231) 830-3700. www.muskegon-heights.k-12.mi.us

Reeths Puffer High School: 1545 Roberts Street. (231) 744-1647. www.reeths-puffer.org

Muskegon Catholic Central High School: 1145 W. Laketon Avenue. (231) 755-2201. www.gmcs.org

Whitehall High School: 3100 White Lake Drive, Whitehall. (231) 893-1020. www.whitehall.k12.mi.us

Montague High School: 4900 Stanton Boulevard, Montague. (231) 894-2661. www.montague.k12.mi.us

Orchard View High School: 16 North Quarterline. (231) 760-1400. www.orchardview.k12.mi.us

North Muskegon High School: 1600 Mills, North Muskegon. (231) 719-4110. www.nmps.k12.mi.us

West Michigan Christian: 455 E. Ellis Road. (231) 799-9644. www.wmchs.net.

Muskegon Community College

Muskegon Community College as it exists today is the result of a long growth process, location changes, and expansion. Its 111-acre campus on Quarterline Road was purchased in September of 1963, but MCC's story begins far earlier.

Founded in 1926 as Muskegon Junior College, the school's first home was the third floor of what was then the new Muskegon High School. By 1934, one building was not enough to house the two institutions, so Muskegon Junior College moved to Hackley School, now the Board of Education Building, in downtown Muskegon. In 1951, the college adopted both a new moniker and a new educational scope. Muskegon Junior College became Muskegon Community College, and with the name change came a variety of new courses meant to serve a larger section of the local populace.

In the years directly preceding the purchase of MCC's present campus, the school was operating full-time from three facilities and part-time from as many as eight other locations. The community then voted to separate the college from the rest of the school system and to fund the construction of what was to become MCC as it is today.

From the construction of the first building in 1967 until the present, Muskegon Community College has grown considerably. The campus now includes the Technology Building, the Hendrik Meijer Library & Information Technology Center, the Bartels-Rode Gymnasium, the Stevenson Center for Higher Education, the Art Building, a planetarium and the Frauenthal Foundation Fine Arts Center, which houses the Overbrook Theater and Art Gallery. Off campus, MCC owns an observatory at the Muskegon Wastewater Management System as well as the University Park Golf Course.

MCC offers a wide variety of courses, including upper level courses and programs presented by Ferris State, Grand Valley State, and Western Michigan universities. Student run media includes MCC-TV Channel 98 and LakeFX online radio. 221 Quarterline Road. Reception Desk: (231) 773-9131. www.muskegoncc.edu or www.lakefxradio.com

Baker College

Baker College of Muskegon got its start more than a century ago in 1888, when Woodbridge Ferris founded the Muskegon College. Across the state, in Flint, Michigan, Eldon Baker had founded Baker Business University. The two institutions were separate until 1965, when a group of Muskegon businessmen represented by Robert Jewell purchased the Flint school and brought both together under a single management. Over the next two decades, the institutions gained accreditation and approval to grant Associates' Degrees in Applied Science and Business, as well as a Bachelor's of Business Administration. In 1990, Muskegon College officially changed its name to Baker College of Muskegon. Presently, Baker College offers a wide variety of programs including culinary arts, elementary and secondary education and computer programming. The college's Michigan Culinary Institute, featuring a restaurant, bakery and pastry shop, will be open to the public in September 2009. Many Baker programs are also available online, as well as at 17 campuses across Michigan. 1903 Marquette Avenue, Muskegon. (231) 777-5200. www.baker.edu

Career Tech Center
At the Muskegon Career Tech Center, 20 programs offer 11th and 12th graders a chance to learn everything from accounting to computer-aided design. Working with local high schools, the Career Tech Center focuses on programs like early childhood education, commercial art, auto body technology, health services, graphic arts, printing, culinary management and horticulture. An extensive counseling program helps match students' abilities and interests with fields that have a promising future. 200 Harvey Street. (231) 767-3600. www.muskegonisd.org/ctc-new/programs

RELIGIOUS LIFE

With over 240 congregations serving a community of 175,000, Muskegon is a great place to sample diverse religious cultures. World-class architecture, fascinating clergy, many special interfaith events, outstanding gospel choirs and a sense of community create opportunities for people with vastly different religious beliefs. Holding them together is a conviction that spiritual worship is central to their everyday lives. While some older mainline congregations have closed, they have been replaced by new non-denominational churches that have recently opened their doors. In some Muskegon and Muskegon Heights neighborhoods, it seems as if there is a church on nearly every street corner. In addition to being home to a wide array of Christian denominations, Muskegon County has a Jewish synagogue, a Unitarian congregation, a Baha'i Peace Park and worshipping congregations of American Muslims and Nation of Islam followers. Here are just a few of the highlights.

Bethesda Baptist Church
The city's oldest continuously worshipping African-American congregation celebrated 97 years in 2007. Originally in downtown Muskegon, they are now located at 575 Getty Street in the Marquette neighborhood. (231) 722-7552.

Annunciation Greek Orthodox Church
This beautiful building on the south end of town, featuring a blue dome, sacred icons and a number of sacred objects in gold, also serves a Romanian Orthodox congregation, which began as a service to refugees. Calling ahead is recommended if you wish to visit. 185 East Pontaluna Road. (231) 799-0185.

St. Francis De Sales Catholic Church
In Norton Shores is an impressive flight of modern design in concrete. One of Muskegon's most recognizable church buildings, it draws students of architecture from around the world. The church has created a walking guide to help visitors appreciate its features. Designed by Marcel Breuer in the 1960s and dedicated in 1967, the building features a soaring sanctuary space and a number of optical illusions. 2929 McCracken Street. (231) 755-1953. A Muskegon Best Bet.

Other Catholic Churches
Each of the Roman Catholic churches in the City of Muskegon was originally centered in an ethnic enclave. **St. Mary's**, at 239 W. Clay Avenue, (231) 722-2844, in downtown

GOSPEL CHOIRS

Many of our African-American congregations are home to excellent music programs, including soul-stirring gospel choirs. Larger congregations include **Bethesda Baptist** at 575 Getty, **Christ Temple Apostolic Church** at 412 E. Sherman in Muskegon Heights, **Church of the Living God** at 4249 South Quarterline in Fruitport Township, **Greater Harvest Missionary Baptist** at 2435 Riordan Street in Muskegon Heights, **Holy Trinity Institutional Church of God in Christ** at 2140 Valley in Muskegon Heights, **Mt. Zion Church of God in Christ** at 188 West Muskegon Avenue in downtown Muskegon, **Philadelphia Missionary Baptist** at 1180 South Getty in Muskegon and **Queen Esther Missionary Baptist** at 2220 Superior in Muskegon Heights.

Muskegon, began as an Irish parish. Their sanctuary was recently refurbished, with beautiful ceiling paintings. **St. Jean Baptiste**, located at 1292 Jefferson, (231) 722-2793, was French. It now offers mass in Spanish every Sunday. **Sacred Heart Church**, 150 E. Summit in Muskegon Heights, (231) 733-2440, was originally Czech, while **St. Michael the Archangel**, 1716 Sixth Street, (231) 722-4666, has Polish roots.

First Congregational Church–United Church of Christ
This church was built with help from many prominent Muskegonites, including Julia Hackley and the Walker family. 1201 Jefferson. (231) 726-3254.

St. Paul's Episcopal Church

St. Paul's, which was supported by Thomas Hume, features a beautiful stained-glass rose window and a large statue of St. Paul overlooking the street. 1006 Third Street. (231) 722-2112.

First Church of Christ Scientist

This Christian Science church features a distinctive dome and white pillars at the entrance. Corner of Third Street and Muskegon Avenue. (231) 722-7704.

Central United Methodist Church

One of Muskegon's largest churches occupies most of a city block in the heart of downtown. Its impressive stained-glass windows were recently refurbished. The colors are spectacular. Bordered by Second and Third Streets and Muskegon and Webster Avenues. (231) 722-6545.

St. Alban's Episcopal Church

In Laketon Township north of North Muskegon, this church has a stone-lined labyrinth in the front lawn. The public is welcome. Take Whitehall Road north to Giles, then turn west toward Lake Michigan. 2065 West Giles Road. (231) 744-1884.

McGraft Memorial Congregational Church

The new building sits above the Ruddiman Creek Lagoon at 1617 Palmer Avenue. (231) 759-0166. The historic Harbor Unitarian Universalist Building at 1296 Montgomery originally served as McGraft Memorial Congregational Church. The McGraft family owned a sawmill in the area of Ruddiman Creek and funded the church.

The **Moses Jones Parkway**, which leads into the City of Muskegon as a connecter to the US 31 expressway, honors a John Wesley African Methodist Episcopal Zion Church pastor who worked tirelessly in the 1960s for racial harmony and equal rights.

Muskegon's **Baha'i Peace Park** is located on Marquette Avenue just a few blocks east of the US 31 business route heading north out of downtown. The parcel has been owned by the Baha'is for over 90 years as a possible future site for a temple. It features a stone representation of the Baha'i nine-pointed star and polished stone benches for contemplation.

For more information about the Muskegon faith community, please contact Muskegon County Cooperating Churches at (231) 727-6000.

ABNER BENNETT'S MUSKEGON MINISTRY

Abner Bennet and his wife, former slaves, founded the Muskegon area Methodist churches. In particular, Montague United Methodist Church, 8555 Cook Street, (231) 894-5789, traces its roots to their ministry work. Mr. Bennett regularly walked from the Montague area, north of White Lake, to the Muskegon settlement to conduct services. Their house, which still stands in the Montague area, is rumored to have been a stop on the Underground Railway, hiding escaped slaves coming up the Lake Michigan shoreline on their way to Canada and freedom.

MUSKEGON'S JEWISH COMMUNITY

Michael Grossman, who grew up in Muskegon, was always proud of his dad's department store, Grossman's, the city's answer to Macy's. "It sponsored the annual Christmas Day Parade and dad, dressed in the store's costume, climbed a fire truck ladder to the roof of the store. From there the Jewish business leader belly laughed and threw candy and toys from his Santa bag to the waving children below."

Although the local Jewish community has just 60 families, it has long played an important role in predominantly Christian Muskegon. The smallest city in the state with a full time rabbi and synagogue, Temple B'nai Israel, Muskegon's Jewish roots go back to the mid-19th century. Tailors, merchants and traveling salesman were followed by department store owners like Grossman who shaped the city's commercial life through their clothing, jewelry and shoe stores, as well as scrap metal businesses, paper companies and auto parts dealerships. From politics to education to the arts, Muskegon's Jewish community has worked hand-in-hand with other faiths to promote racial tolerance, serve the less fortunate and develop the city's considerable resources. Pulling together in times of crisis is an old story in smaller communities, and crossing boundaries to spread joy in the grand manner of Herman Grossman is a good example of the city's interfaith brotherhood. If the spirit moves you, feel free to stop by **Temple B'Nai Israel** on a Friday night to sample this rich and enduring tradition. 391 West Webster Avenue. (231) 722-2702.

MUSKEGON'S ECONOMY

Muskegon's economy has always been tied to its natural resources. In the beginning, commerce was defined as fur trading between the French explorers and the Native Americans. Then the vast forested lands were harvested for lumber. It was the lumbering era that put Muskegon on the map, providing jobs for thousands of men immigrating to this country. Michigan's great white pine helped to rebuild Chicago after the Great Fire of 1871. When community leaders accepted the fact that the renewable resource of trees would take generations to replenish, they set out to attract industry to Muskegon.

The Muskegon Area Chamber of Commerce led an effort to lure the young manufacturing industries of the larger cities to this picturesque community. After much trial and error, the strong manufacturing sector was born, and much of it is still thriving today. Industrialists discovered that the freshwater sand dunes produced high quality castings to be used for making metal. Muskegon became known throughout the world as the place to find superior metal parts for automotive, aerospace, medical, machinery and many other products. Production during war times was critical to the national defense effort. Simultaneously, the manufacturing of wood products such as furniture began to thrive, as did plastics and food processing.

Today you will find such companies as Alcoa Howmet, Eagle Alloy, CWC Textron, Port City Group, Knoll and Hines Corporation. Cole's Quality Foods is here baking their famous garlic bread. Saga cheese is produced in Norton Shores, and nearby is Gerber Baby Food.

Muskegon has become the West Michigan lakeshore hub for health care, services and retail outlets providing thousands of jobs for area residents. With the higher education facilities of Baker College, Muskegon Community College and Grand Valley State University, educators may find employment as well. The community college has extension programs with Ferris State University, Michigan State University and Western Michigal University.

It has only been in that last decade that tourism has evolved to become a major player in the local economy, thanks to the millions of dollars invested in the growth of Michigan's Adventure, the *Lake Express* ferry and the numerous arts and cultural attractions including museums and educational facilities—and the Internet, which has helped world travelers to discover the beautiful beaches on Michigan's West Coast.

ON THE JOB IN MUSKEGON COUNTY

Although most visitors know Muskegon for its recreational communities, this is also a good place to work. With 85,000 jobs and a mean family income of $52,000, Muskegon County is home to major employers including Alcoa's Howmet Division, which makes key engine parts for just about every plane in the sky. Other major employers like CWC Textron and Dana Corporation supply the auto industry and Knoll is a well known furniture manufacturer. L-3 Communications focuses on Abrams Tank components for the military. The city is also host to a number of chemical companies such as Sun.

While Muskegon was traditionally a lumbering and manufacturing center, only the city's Sappi Fine Paper Mill and two foundries remain. Light manufacturing, the tourist industry, two major hospitals, correctional facilities, a burgeoning retail sector at the Lakes Mall and a reborn downtown are now all central to the region's economy. In addition the city's arts and entertainment community continues to attract new talent. Ambiance and affordability are all part of the draw.

Technology has allowed Muskegon to become popular with "remote workers." These people work out of their homes for global employers thanks to the accessibility of high-speed Internet throughout the county. They can live on the water affordably and nurture their career or small business.

A new generation of telecommuters who work for national companies from a Muskegon base is another important economic asset for this growing populace. They love the convenience of the Muskegon airport, a nice alternative to crowded hub terminals.

MUSKEGON COUNTY REAL ESTATE

Unless you are determined to live on Lake Michigan or one of the city's popular recreation lakes, chances are you will find real estate in Muskegon an enticing opportunity. Here you will quickly discover many good deals in neighborhoods offering great schools, convenient shopping, easy waterfront access and a good quality of life. A convenient way to get started is to simply pick up the *Muskegon Chronicle* on Sunday or one of the local housing guides. From modestly priced fixer-uppers to recently built homes with an acre or two of land, the county is a great place for a young family or someone looking to ease into a comfortable retirement. If you're coming from a large urban area, you'll be glad to know that many fine homes in the Muskegon area sell for well under $200,000. With an average home resale listing price of $159,000, it's no surprise that 77 percent of the county's families own their own homes. Those looking for starter homes can find plenty of good buys under $100,000. Depending on your needs, you'll find good values across the county, from the small town ambience of Whitehall and Montague to downtown condo living in Muskegon.

If you prefer apartment living or the rental housing market, don't think twice. This is an ideal way to get to know the area and ultimately decide where you want to buy. There are plenty of move-in allowances and special deals in first-rate areas.

Because the community does have schools of choice, families aren't necessarily limited by school district boundaries. If you're a first-time buyer in the area, do yourself a favor. Spend some time driving or even biking around and taking a look at recreation opportunities, traffic patterns and, of course, nearby shopping. Because there is no significant traffic congestion in the area, drives of more than 30 minutes are rare, and most destinations can be easily reached in 15 minutes.

If you choose to go upscale and look for waterfront property, you will also have plenty of choices. Unlike other parts of the country, you probably can be patient and maybe even a little picky. If you are moving from a higher cost of living area, it's likely that you will be surprised by the quantity and quality available. Looking with a good local realtor always make sense. When you're on your search, it's good to keep in mind that this market is ideal for families that want to stable a horse, purchase a house with a pool or find a place that backs up on to a river. If you love cross-country skiing, biking, Frisbee golf, tennis, shuffleboard, basketball or kayaking, you should easily find a house within five to ten minutes of these sports. Large lot sizes in many areas are ideal for those who want to have their own vegetable or herb garden. Not sold yet? Simply try a few open houses and you'll see why Muskegon continues to attract new families from all over the country.

ACKNOWLEDGEMENTS

All opinions expressed in *Muskegon 365* are those of the writers and editors. The Muskegon Convention and Visitors Bureau, the Muskegon Chamber of Commerce, the Muskegon Community Foundation, the White Lake Area Chamber of Commerce and the Community Foundation of Muskegon all contributed their expertise to this project. None of the businesses or venues recommended in *Muskegon 365* paid for placement. The researchers and writers paid their own way, from state park fees to the roller coasters of Michigan's Adventure.

Many people made tireless contributions to this project, including Cindy Larsen, Jill Foreman, Sam Wendling, Amy Van Loon and the staff at RDR Books. We also gratefully acknowledge Dan Royer and the writing department at Grand Valley State University. Interns from GVSU did excellent research and writing for this project. Jeff Alexander at the *Muskegon Chronicle* lent his insider's knowledge of the fishing scene, and we are also grateful to Delphine Hogston for her work on the churches section, Ric Pedler for his work on the birding section, and Elizabeth Brockwell-Tillman, who did the flora and fauna feature. Special thanks to Sarah Meinel, a writer with a bright future, who did excellent work on this project. In addition, Megan Trank, RDR's secret weapon, was extremely helpful. In the center of the storm, Colleen Weesies and Kellie Norman were invaluable. We also acknowledge our managing editor, Richard Harris, one of the nation's leading travel writers and editors, who brought his professionalism to this project.

CONTRIBUTORS

Author **Roger Rapoport**, a Muskegon native, has written, co-written or edited numerous travel guidebooks, as well as other journalistic nonfiction books including *Hillsdale: Greek Tragedy in America's Heartland*. His most recent work, *Citizen Moore: The Making of an American Iconoclast*, won the 2007 *ForeWord Magazine* Book of the Year Gold Award for Biography.

Elizabeth Brockwell-Tillman is the director of the Gillette Sand Dune Visitor Center and head naturalist at P.J. Hoffmaster State Park.

Book and cover designer **Richard Harris** is the managing editor of RDR Books and the author of more than 40 travel guidebooks.

Writer/researcher **Louis Jeannot**, a graduate of Kalamazoo College, is a graphic designer and webmaster for RDR Books.

Writer/researcher **Laura Mazade** holds a degree from the Writing Department at Michigan's Grand Valley State University.

Researcher **Rowena McKenzie** is a graduate of Grand Valley State University living in Grand Rapids.

Associate editor **Sarah Meinel** lives in Grand Haven, Michigan. She obtained a B.A. in Psychology from the University of Michigan and is a social worker by day.

Researcher **Rachel Moblo** is a student at Michigan State University. She lives in Lansing.

Kellie Norman is RDR Books' office manager. She grew up in Muskegon and returned to the city after living and working in Florida. She lives near one of the city's Best Bets, Hoffmaster State Park.

Researcher **Jessi Prouse** is a student at Grand Valley State University.

Photographer **Dan Rapoport** has served as president of the Muskegon Camera Club. He has been photographing in the Muskegon area for over 60 years.

Writer/researcher **Mike Schertenlieb** lives in Muskegon.

Writer/researcher **Abby Schmeling**, a graduate of Grand Valley State University, lives in Grand Rapids and works in the RDR Books marketing department.

Writer/researcher **Sarah Sheehan** is a graduate of Grand Valley State University.

Associate editor **Megan Trank**, a longtime Muskegon resident, is a graduate of Smith College. She presently works for the Right to Write Foundation, an organization dedicated to defending the First Amendment rights of authors and other creative artists.

Writer/researcher **Colleen Weesies**, a lifelong resident of the White Lake area, has served as office manager of RDR Books and is presently a consultant to the company.

INDEX

Above and Beyond 163
Addiction Charters 102
Airport Antiques Mall 127
air travel 10
Alcoa Howmet 184, 185
Alexander, Dave 15
Alexander, Jeff 15, 68, 101
All American Girls
  Professional Baseball
  League 82
Alley Door Club 105
Alpine Motel 29
Amazon Knitting Company
  19
AMF Muskegon Lanes 90
Amtrak 11, 12
Annis Water Resources
  Institute 47-48
Annunciation Greek Orthodox
  Church 178
Art Cats Gallery 94, 131
Art's Steelhead Charters 102
ArtWorks 47

Baker College 47, 134, 175,
  184
Baha'i Peace Park 181
Barnes & Noble 131
Barry's Flower Shop and
  Greenhouses 155
Bat'n Club Mini Golf 90
Baymont 21, 26

Beachwood Park 53
Bear Lake Tavern 107
beer tents 120
Bel-Aire Motel 28
Bellacino's 138
Bennett, Abner 181
Bent Pine Golf Club 88
Benton Harbor, MI 9
Bernie O's 138
Best Western Inn and Suites
  27
Bethany Christian Reformed
  Church 159
Bethesda Baptist Church 178,
  179
bicycle rentals 12
Bienvenue Antiques 127
Big Blue Lake 59
Big Rigs . . . Big Party West
  Michigan Truck Show 119
bike trails 65
birding 70-75
Blessing of the Boats 115
Blue Lake County Park 59-60
Blue Lake Fine Arts Camp 6,
  20
Bluffton Bay Marina 103
boat launch raps 104
B.O.B. (Grand Rapids) 110
Bobarinos (Grand Rapids)
  111
Bob Ely's Kountry Kamping 62

Bob Hi Lanes 91
Book Nook and Java Shop
    131
bowling 90
Bridgeton 69
Bronson Beach 55
Brooklyn Bagels 135
Brownstone 138
bus travel 11
Butler, John 78

Camera Store 129
camping 57–62
canoeing 68-70
Captain Jack's 55
Career Tech Center 176
Carmen's Café and Mercantile
    139
car rentals 11-12
Carter, James 6
Casnovia 85
Causeway Bay Motel 30
Cedar Creek Motorsport Trail
    67
Central Paper Company 19
Central United Methodist
    Church 157, 180
C.F. Prime Chophouse &
    Wine Bar 139
Chase Hammond Golf Club
    88
Chase Piano Company 19
Cheese Lady, The 50
Cherokee Restaurant 20, 139
Chicago, IL 9, 10, 11, 12, 13, 14

Chippewa Indians 33
Christ Temple Apostolic
    Church 179
Church of the Living God
    179
Cinema Carousel Theatre 113
City of Muskegon Leisure
    Services 52
City Café 42, 139
Clay Avenue Cellars 44-45,
    132
Claybanks Pottery 132
Clipper Cup 97
Coastline Deli 140
Cocoa Cottage Bed and
    Breakfast 22
Coffee House 136
Colby Street Shops Antique
    Mall 152
Cole's Quality Foods 184
Comerica Village Craft
    Market 118
Comfort Inn 21, 27
Continental Motors 19
Coopersville 109
Coopersville Farm Museum
    109
Corner House of Gifts 152
Country Dairy, Inc. & Farm
    Store 84
Craig's Cruisers Family Fun
    Center 83, 90
Creswick Farms 84
Cross-n-Creek Campground
    62

Croton Dam 68, 101
Croton Dam Float Trips 69
Crush (Grand Rapids) 111
Cruzin' White Lake 121
Custer Park 164
Cuti's Sports Bar & Grill 107
CWC Textron 184, 185

Dana Corporation 185
Dave's Harvest 85
Derbyshire Renaissane Faire
    116
Details and Design 50
Depot-to-Depot Tour 62
Deremo Access Site 104
Detroit, MI 9, 12, 13
Dewey Sailboat Charters 98
Dockers Fish House and
    Lounge 20, 56, 136, 140
Dockside Grill 98
Dog 'N Suds 148
Dog Star Ranch 26
Double JJ Ranch & Golf
    Resort 85, 119
Downtown Muskegon 5, 21,
    24, 32-50, 110, 115, 117,
    119
Dr. Grins (Grand Rapids) 111
Duck Lake State Park 20, 30,
    60, 63, 67, 104, 109
Dune Climb Stairway 57

Eagle Alloy 184
Eagle Island Golf Club 88
East Lansing, MI 13

Edison Landing 48
El Camino Taco 148
Elliot, Margaret Drake 56, 76
El Tapatio 20, 140
Eve (Grand Rapids) 111

Fairfield, Shane 78
Fairfield Inn and Suites 21,
    25
Family Christian Bookstore
    131
ferry travel 10-11
Fiesta Sabor Latino 115
Finch Nest, A 23, 160
Fire Barn Museum 41
First Church of Christ
    Scientist 159, 180
First Congregational Church–
    United Church of Christ
    158, 179
Fisherman's Landing 61
fishing 69, 98-103
Fishtail Charters 102
Fitzgerald, Edward 33
Forest Park Covenant Church
    158
Frauenthal Center for
    the Performing Arts
    (Frauenthal Theater) 6, 20,
    24, 42, 47, 95, 111, 112,
    114-115, 116, 123, 124,
    139, 142, 163, 172
Frauenthal Jefferson Home
    123
Fremont 62, 86, 87

Frey Foundation 47
Fricano's 141
Frosty Oasis 148
Fruitport 23, 121
Fruitport Golf Club 88

Gerber Baby Food 184
Getty 4 Drive-in Theatre 113
Ghezzi's Market 94-95
G & L Chili Dogs 146
Glenside Café 141
Glenside Pub 107, 141
Go Gear Outdoors 133
golf 87-90
Goodgrains Bake House 135
Grand Haven 72, 110
Grand Rapids, MI 9, 10, 11, 12, 13, 14, 47, 110-111
Grand Rapids Press 15
Grand Traverse Pie Company 141
Grand Valley State University 47, 184
Granholm, Jennifer 49
Greater Harvest Missionary Baptist Church 179
Greater Muskegon Historic Association 49
Greater Muskegon Women's Club 162
Great Lakes Guide Service 102
Great Lakes Java Co. 136
Great Lakes Marina and Boat Sales 103

Great Lakes Naval Memorial and Museum 46, 64, 115
Greyhound 11
Grossman, Michael 182
Grossman's 182
Grimette, Mark 64
Gurney Park 66

Hackley, Charles 18-19, 33, 38, 43
Hackley & Hume Historic Sites 6, 24, 40-41, 47, 64, 130
Hackley Hospital 16, 19
Hackley Park 39, 43, 47, 115, 117, 118
Hackley Public Library 5, 7, 19, 20, 24, 33, 36, 38, 47, 51, 63
Haglund, Kristen 116
Hampton Inn 25
Happy Mohawk Canoe Livery 61, 69, 101
Harbor Steakhouse 141
Harbor Theater 93, 94, 113
Harbor Town Yacht Club 161
Hardiman, Clayton 15
Hart 66, 86
Hart-Montague Trail State Park 65, 67
Hearthstone Restaurant 20, 142
Hegg's Furniture Gallery 50
Henrickson, Dan 48
Heritage Farms and Market 87

Heritage Holiday Home Tour 123
Heritage Landing 43-44, 48, 117, 123, 165
Heritage Memorial Garden 44, 164
Hickory Knoll Golf Course 88
hiking trails 65
Hines Corporation 184
Hobo's Tavern 107, 142
Hoffmaster State Park 5, 23, 26, 56-57, 67, 72
Holiday Festival of Trees 124
Holiday Inn Muskegon Harbor 21, 24, 51, 110, 141
Holland, MI 11, 14, 47
Holton 62
Holy Trinity Institutional Church of God in Christ 179
Hopkins, David S. 40
Horseshoe and Holton Motorcycle Trails 67
Hot Rod Harley-Davidson 50
House of Chan 148
Howmet Playhouse 20, 23, 112-113
Huntington Bank Bistro 119
Hyatt Blueberry Farm 85

Iddings, Bill 15

Jilly's Gallery 49, 132

Joe's Steak House 148
Johnson Pavilion 44
Jumpin' Jupiter Skating Center 83

kayaking 68-70, 133
Keaton, Buster 95
Keefe's Pharmacy 123
Keep, Paul 15
Kingsley, Bob 100
Kirby Grill (Grand Haven) 110
kites 66
kite surfing 66
Klinefelter's Gallery 152
Knoll Inc. 184
KOA of Muskegon 62
Kolb, David 15
Kruse Park 55, 72
Kruse Park Dog Run 26

Lake Express 5, 10-11, 14, 93, 184
Lake Fran Campground 62
Lake Harbor Park 53, 73
Lake Michigan 2, 3, 5, 22, 23, 24, 28, 30, 31, 53, 57, 58, 59, 60, 62, 66, 76, 97, 99, 100, 101, 117, 151, 152, 161, 186
Lake Michigan Center 49
Lake Sch-Nepp-A-Ho 61
Lakeshore Marketplace 128
Lakeshore Sports Centre 81, 83

Lakeshore Tavern 107
Lakeshore Trail 65, 93, 117
Lakeside District 93-95, 131
Lakeside Dune Glass 94
Lakeside Emporium 95
Lakeside Inn 30, 136, 150, 161
Lakes Mall 25, 28, 29, 83, 128, 135, 138, 141, 185
Landmark Bar & Grill
Lane's Landing 71, 72
Langeland House 160
Lansing, MI 9
L.C. Walker Arena 78, 79, 83, 142
Lee & Birch 129
Lewis' Farm Market and Petting Zoo 85-86
Lipka's Old Fashioned Soda Fountain 152
Lisman, Tony 78
Little Flower Creek 59
Local Pub 108
lodging 21-31
Loop to Loop Trail 58
Lorenz, Tracy 15
Lost Boat Ceremony 46, 115
Lost Lake 58, 71
Lost Treasures of the Great Lakes 94
Lothschutz Farms 86
LST-393 45, 115, 160
L-3 Communications 185

Mackinaw Kites and Toys 66

Magicland Farms 86
Main Street Mardi Gras Pub Crawl 110
Main Street Pub & Eatery 137
Mango's 142
Manistee National Forest 6, 67
Maple Tree Inn 28
Maranatha Bible and Missionary Conference Center 21, 31
Margaret Drake Elliot Park 56
Margie J Sport Fishing Charters 102
Marine Tap Room 108
Master Gardeners of Muskegon 43, 164
McDonalds Homemade Candies and Coffee Shop 130
McGraft Memorial Congregational Church 180
McGraft Park 54
Medbury Park 151
Meijer Art in the Park 118
Meijers 147
Meinert County Park 59
Mercy Health Partners 17, 123
Mesaba Airlines 3, 10
Michigan Alternative and Renewable Energy Center 48

Michigan Audubon Society 70
Michigan City, IN 10, 13
Michigan Culinary Institute 32, 47, 49, 134, 175
Michigan Irish Music Festival 44, 123
Michigan Marketplace 118
Michigan Training and Education Center 173
Michigan's Adventure 25, 27, 29, 30, 59, 61, 62, 115, 166-171, 184
Michillinda Lodge 21, 30, 108, 137, 150, 161
Mike's Landing 143
Milwaukee, WI 5, 12, 14
Milwaukee Clipper 45-46, 115
Miss Michigan Pageant 116
Mona Lake Park 54, 136
Mona Lake Channel 53, 73
Mona Shores High School 124, 172, 173
Mona Shores High School Singing Christmas Tree 124, 172
Monet Garden 43, 164
Montague 25, 29, 63, 69, 72, 87, 89, 100, 104, 121, 131, 133, 148, 150-155, 161, 181
Montague High School 173
Montague Tree Farms 87
Montague Bicycle Trail 29

Montague Mountain Inn 28-29
Moose Fest 122
Moses Jones Parkway 181
Moss Ridge Golf Club 88, 163
Mr. B's Pancake House 143
Mt. Zion Church of God in Christ 159, 179
Muskegon Antique Mall 127
Muskegon Area Chamber of Commerce 16, 19, 33, 36, 183
Muskegon Area District Libraries 51
Muskegon Area Transit System 12
Muskegon Big Reds 77
Muskegon Bike Time 108, 121
Muskegon Charter Boat Association 99
Muskegon Chronicle 6, 14-15, 56, 68, 100, 186
Muskegon Civic Theatre 112
Muskegon Community College 174-175, 184
Muskegon Community Concerts 111
Muskegon Community Foundation 19, 33, 43
Muskegon Community Health Project 149
Muskegon Conservation Club 71

Muskegon Country Club 87, 162
Muskegon County 7
Muskegon County Airport 10, 25, 28, 29, 139
Muskegon County Convention and Visitor's Bureau 15, 36
Muskegon County Fair 121
Muskegon County Fairgrounds 116, 121
Muskegon County Museum & Mercantile 6, 24, 39, 40, 130
Muskegon County Museum of African American History 39
Muskegon County Nature Club 70
Muskegon Department of Leisure Services 52, 55
Muskegon Elks Lodge 274 Park 62
Muskegon Farmers and Flea Market 125
Muskegon Film Festival 114-115
Muskegon Fury 20, 78, 79
Muskegon Heights 54, 116, 177
Muskegon Heights Farmers Market 126
Muskegon Heights Festival in the Park 116
Muskegon Heights High School 77, 172, 173
Muskegon High School 172, 173
Muskegon Lake 63, 69, 71, 93, 97, 100, 104, 109, 136, 137, 161, 164, 165
Muskegon Lake Channel 56, 71, 72
Muskegon Lake Nature Preserve 71
Muskegon Lake State Park 44, 48, 54, 57-58, 109
Muskegon Main Street Car & Motorcycle Show 116
Muskegon Museum of Art 5-6, 20, 24, 37, 124
Muskegon Railroad Historical Society 40
Muskegon River 68, 69, 73, 85, 99
Muskegon River Causeway 63, 71
Muskegon Sandbox 91
Muskegon Shoreline Spectacular 122
Muskegon State Game Area 72
Muskegon State Park 5, 29, 57-58, 60, 63, 67, 71
Muskegon Summer Celebration 7, 44, 117-119, 120
Muskegon Technical Academy 173
Muskegon Thunder 78, 79

Muskegon Trolley Company 36, 80, 165
Muskegon Wastewater Management System 71, 73, 74-75, 174
Muskegon Winter Sports Complex 20, 48, 58, 67, 79
Muskegon Yacht Club 98
Muskegon Zonta Club 164
Musketawa Trail 65, 67

National Pro Hill Climb 91
Navi-Gater Charters 102
Nelson Neighborhood Association 123
Newaygo 68, 101
New Era 84, 85, 86, 132
North Muskegon 29, 63, 71, 91, 100, 102, 104, 106, 107, 130, 135, 138, 142, 143, 149, 155, 164
North Muskegon Charters 102
North Muskegon High School 173
North Shore Books 130
Northside 138, 145
Northway Lanes & Billiards 91
Norton Shores 25, 54, 113
Nuthatch, The 70
Nuveen Center for the Arts 153

Oak Knoll Family Campground 62
Oak Ridge Golf Course 89
Oat Bran Boys 109
Old Channel Trail Golf Course 89, 162
Old Indian Cemetery 49
Orchard View Day Camp 81
Orchard View High School 173
Osgood, Sidney J. 36
Ottawa Indians 33

Pablo's 149
Page's 153
Paisley Place, The 153
parks 52-60
Parsley's Sport Shop 101
Parties in the Park 110, 120
Pere Marquette Park/Beach 20, 26, 53, 55, 56, 72, 100, 122
Philadelphia Missionary Baptist Church 179
Pigs Eye Guide Service
Pines Motel 29
Pints & Quarts 108, 143
Pioneer County Park 58
Pita Place 143
Pitkin's Drug and Gift Shoppe 123, 153
Plumb's 147
Plumb's Annual Picnic 119
Pomona Park 23
Pop, Iggy 105

Poppen, Sherman 92
Port City Group 184
Port City Princess 20, 45, 96, 160
Port City Victorian Inn 22, 159
Portobello (Grand Haven) 110
Powers Outdoors 69, 133
Pringle, Don 78
public transportation 9-12
Putters Creek Mini-Golf 90

Queen Esther Missionary Baptist Church 179

Racquets Downtown Grill 51, 143
Radium Photo 129
Rafferty's 137
Rainbow Ranch Horseback Riding Stables 84
Ramada Inn—Whitehall 27
Ramsay, Bruce 78
Ravenna 89, 102
Ravenna Creeks Golf Course 89
Ravenna Sewage Ponds 73
Raymor Fish Products 103
Ream, Patti 152
Red Rooster 109
Reeths Puffer High School 172, 173
Rennhack Orchards Market 86

River Rat Canoe Rentals 70
Rock the Coast 115
Rocky Point Mini-Golf 90, 171
Roller Fox 83
Roosevelt Park 109, 135, 139, 143
Rose Bud Bar & Grille (Grand Haven) 110
Ross Park 54
Rothbury 85, 91, 119-120
Ruddiman Creek 54
Run-N-Gun Charters 102
Ruth Ann's Ice Cream 58, 149
Ryerson, Martin 49
Ryke's Bakery and Café 144

Sacred Heart Catholic Church 179
Saga Cheese 184
sailing 97-98
St. Alban's Episcopal Church 180
St. Francis De Sales Catholic Church 47, 158, 178
St. Jean Baptiste Catholic Church 157, 179
St. Mary's Catholic Church 178
St. Michael the Archangel Catholic Church 179
St. Paul's Episcopal Church 157, 180
Salvation Army Day Camp 82

Sam's Bistro 113, 144
Sappi Fine Paper Mill 185
Sardine Room 20, 144
Scolnik House 41, 123
Seaway Run 117
750 Grill 105, 137
Seyferth Park 53
Sherman Bowling Center & Billiards 91
Shoreline Inn and Suites 21, 24
Shoreline Service Bait and Tackle 100
Snug Harbor 58, 63, 71, 100
Snug Harbor Bait Shop 100
Snug Harbor Motel 29
Soldiers & Sailors Monument 43
Sorry Charlie Charters 98
South Bend, IN 9, 14
South Shore Marina 98, 101
Speck, Scott 111
Spring Lake 23, 83
SS *Badger* 11
Starbucks 135
Station Grill 144-145
Steak N Egger 145
Stonegate Golf Club 89
Sun Wind and Rain 49
Sweetwater Local Foods Market 126-127

Taste of Muskegon 117
taxis 12
Temple B'nai Israel 158, 182

Terrace Plaza 47, 140
Terrace Point 24
Tipsy Toad 109, 110
Toast'n Jam's Restaurant 145
Tony's Bistro 145
Torrent House 47
Torresen Marine 20, 97, 103
Through the Looking Glass 94, 132
Thunderbird Race Park 91
train travel 11
Trailway Campground 62
Trillium Banquet and Catering 163
Trillium Festival 57
Twin Lake 86, 89

Union Depot 15, 36, 63, 123
Unity Christian Music Festival 44, 122
University Park Golf Course 89, 174
USCGC McLane W-146 46
USS *Silversides* 46, 115
US-31 BBQ 146
Utopian Marketplace 154

Veterans Memorial Park 71
Victory Inn and Suites 29
Village Park Bed and Breakfast 23

Walker Community Center 164
Warmington, Steve 108

Wasserman's Floral 129
WaterMark Center 123
Wayne's Deli & Beverage 129, 146
WBLV-FM 6
Weathervane Inn 24-25, 161
weddings 156-165
Weesies Brothers Farms, Inc. 154
Wesco 147
West Coast Carriage Company 37, 165
West Shore Symphony Orchestra 111
West Wind Golf Course 90
West Marine 133
West Michigan Christian High School 77, 173
West Michigan Concert WINDS 112
West Michigan Yacht Charters, LLC 97
Whippy Dip 149
Whitehall 22, 23, 27, 28, 30, 31, 60, 63, 72, 85, 98, 100, 101, 108, 121, 127, 136, 137, 144, 146, 150-155, 160, 162
Whitehall High School 173
White Lake 2, 21, 24, 31, 62, 136, 150-155, 161
White Lake Boat Ramp 104

White Lake Beacon 14
White Lake Chamber of Commerce 64, 150
White Lake Channel 72, 100, 151
White Lake Community Library 51, 66, 151
White Lake Country Club 73
White Lake Depot 63
White Lake Greenouse 154
White River 20, 61, 69, 100
White River Campground 61, 101
White River Gallery 153
White River Light Station Museum 30, 63, 64, 151
White River Marsh 72
White River Nature Trail 63
White Swan Bed and Breakfast 22
WildWater Adventure 166-171
windsurfing 66
Windy Pines 87
Winston Motor Speedway 91
Wishes & Watercolors 132
Wisner Canoe Rental 69, 101
Wolffis, Susan Harrison 15
Wolf Lake Resort and Campground 62

YMCA 7, 48, 80, 117